# The Reception of Unconventional Science

# AAAS Selected Symposia Series

Published by Westview Press
5500 Central Avenue, Boulder, Colorado

for the

American Association for the Advancement of Science
1776 Massachusetts Ave., N.W., Washington, D.C.

# The Reception of Unconventional Science

Edited by Seymour H. Mauskopf

AAAS Selected Symposium 25

*AAAS Selected Symposia Series*

Copyright © 1979 by the American Association for the
Advancement of Science

Published in 1979 in the United States of America by
    Westview Press, Inc.
    5500 Central Avenue
    Boulder, Colorado  80301
    Frederick A. Praeger, Publisher

Library of Congress Catalog Card Number:  78-19735
ISBN: 0-89158-297-5

Printed and bound in the United States of America

# About the Book

The issue of perhaps greatest concern to historians of
science today is the internalist-externalist dichotomy.
This volume directly addresses that issue, at the same time
providing a context for the serious study of heterodox science
and scientific theories. The book consists of four studies,
each of which considers the response of a scientific community
to an unconventional theory or claim: the acausal physics
of Heisenberg; Wegener's geological theory of continental
drift; acupuncture; and the statistical argument for extra-
sensory perception. As they reveal a wide range of reactions
to orthodoxy, the studies themselves exemplify the range of
approaches the historian may use in examining scientific
unconventionality.

# About the Series

The *AAAS Selected Symposia Series* was begun in 1977 to provide a means for more permanently recording and more widely disseminating some of the valuable material which is discussed at the AAAS Annual National Meetings. The volumes in this *Series* are based on symposia held at the Meetings which address topics of current and continuing significance, both within and among the sciences, and in the areas in which science and technology impact on public policy. The *Series* format is designed to provide for rapid dissemination of information, so the papers are not typeset but are reproduced directly from the camera-copy submitted by the authors, without copy editing. The papers are organized and edited by the symposium arrangers who then become the editors of the various volumes. Most papers published in this *Series* are original contributions which have not been previously published, although in some cases additional papers from other sources have been added by an editor to provide a more comprehensive view of a particular topic. Symposia may be reports of new research or reviews of established work, particularly work of an interdisciplinary nature, since the AAAS Annual Meetings typically embrace the full range of the sciences and their societal implications.

WILLIAM D. CAREY
*Executive Officer*
*American Association for*
*the Advancement of Science*

# Contents

# About the Editor and Authors

*Seymour H. Mauskopf, associate professor in the Department of History at Duke University, specializes in history of science, particularly of 18th and 19th century physical science, and of parapsychology.  A member of the History of Science Society, he is the author of a monograph entitled* Crystals and Compounds: Molecular Structure and Composition in Nineteenth Century French Science *(Trans. Amer. Phil. Soc., Vol. 66, Pt. 3, 1976), and articles on the history of 18th and 19th century chemistry and on the history of parapsychology.*

*John Z. Bowers, president of the Josiah Macy, Jr. Foundation, is a specialist in internal medicine.  He is president of the National Omega Alpha Honor Medical Society and is a Chevalier of The Legion of Homor of France (1975).  He is the author of several books on medicine in the Orient, including* Western Medical Pioneers in Feudal Japan *(Johns Hopkins, 1970) and* Western Medicine in a Chinese Palace: Peking Union Medical College, 1917-1951 *(Josiah Macy, Jr. Foundation, 1972).*

*Paul Forman, curator of modern physics at the National Museum of History and Technology of the Smithsonian Institution, is a specialist in the history of physics in the 20th century.  He is coauthor of* Physics circa 1900 *(with J.L. Heilbron and S. Weast; Princeton Univ. Press, 1975) and has published articles on various aspects of physics and scientific activities in Germany in the 1920s.*

*Henry R. Frankel, associate professor of philosophy at the University of Missouri-Kansas City, has been studying why one scientific theory is accepted over another.  He is currently preparing an historical and philosophical analysis of continental drift theory under a National Science Foundation grant, has written several articles on the subject applying Laudan's analysis of scientific growth and change, and has analyzed the developments in terms of Imre Lakatos' account.*

*Michael R. McVaugh, professor in the Department of History at the University of North Carolina, is an historian of science.  He has served on the council of the History of Science Society and was advisory editor of* Isis *from 1972 to 1977.  His background article on psychical research before J.B. Rhine's work on extra-sensory perception was published in* Isis *in 1976.*

*Marcello Truzzi, professor and head of the Department of Sociology at Eastern Michigan University, has conducted research on various aspects of sociology, including folklore and the sociology of the arts, of popular culture, and of parapsychology and deviant sciences.  He has also studied various aspects of the occult.  A member of numerous professional organizations, he is the editor of* Zetetic Scholar *and former editor of* The Zetetic *(the Journal of the Committee for the Scientific Investigation of Claims of the Paranormal). He has published numerous articles and edited over ten books in these fields, most recently,* Solving Social Problems: The Relevance of Sociology *(Goodyear, 1975).*

# The Reception of Unconventional Science

# Introduction

Seymour H. Mauskopf

This volume presents four studies of the
reception of unconventional science.  The appella-
tion "unconventional" has been chosen purposely to
cover a spectrum of innovations or heterodoxies
ranging from some which have long since become
fully normalized in science to others which
remain problematical to most scientists.  The
four cases are: the reception of acausal physics
by German and British physicists in the mid- and
late-1920's; the reception of continental drift
theory by geologists; the reception of acupuncture
by western and western-trained physicians; and the
reception of parapsychology by American psychologists and statisticians in the mid-1930's.  The
first two cases clearly represent normalized
science (although only recently for continental
drift theory); regarding the latter two, it is
still highly uncertain what their ultimate scientific status will be.

The interest among historians, philosophers
and sociologists of science in the process of the
reception of unconventional science has been a
long standing one, but it was undoubtedly brought
to a focus by T. S. Kuhn's The Structure of Scientific Revolution,[1] a book whose raison d'être was
the study of scientific change.  Kuhn took explicit issue with traditional cumulative views of
scientific advance and proposed instead a picture
of science in which the course of scientific
development is from time to time punctuated by
episodes of "crisis" or "revolution" which alter

the entire fabric of a science. More specifically,
in periods of crisis, a scientific community wit-
nesses a challenge to its hitherto dominant, con-
trolling system of scientific theory and method--
its "paradigm," in Kuhn's term--by an upstart,
rival and in many ways, incommensurable paradigm.
The cause of crisis was conventionally enough
ascribed by Kuhn to the buildup of empirical
anomalies but he was less conventional (and less
clear) about how such crises become resolved.
Indeed, with suggestions that the switch in
allegiance on the part of scientists from an old
to a new paradigm was like a "conversion" or that
the emergence of conflicting paradigms was analo-
gous to the polarization of a community preceding
and during a revolution (in the political and
social sense), Kuhn opened himself to the charge
of advocating an irrational view of scientific
change.

Kuhn's scheme for scientific development and
change has produced relatively few specific
applications to historical cases by historians of
science, perhaps because his monograph was only a
sketch and many of its critical concepts left
vague or slippery in meaning, as his critics have
pointed out. It has produced a much richer, if
more pungently critical literature among philosophers of science.[2] Philosophy of science had
already begun to move beyond its traditional
ahistorical mode of analysis towards a more historically modulated concentration on the process of
change. Kuhn's work fell therefore on attuned, if
not necessarily sympathetic ears. Also, although
the original version of Kuhn's book was markedly
"internalist" in orientation, concentrating mainly
on paradigms as intellectual systems, implicit in
his model of the history of science was a sociological undergird: science was an activity carried
on by communities of scientists; paradigms were
those systems of thought and method held by particular communities and indeed, "learned" in the
process of professional training; "revolutions"
were won when the bulk of a scientific community
accepted a new paradigm. In The Structure of
Scientific Revolutions, Kuhn had opined that the
nature of scientific communities had yet to be
analyzed and delineated but a start was certainly
being made with the development of the sociology

of science in the early 1960's and subsequently.[3]

Kuhn's repudiation of a cumulative view of scientific development raised insistent questions about the meaning of scientific "progress" or, to put it somewhat differently, about whether it was possible to establish criteria for judging the superiority of a victorious paradigm over its competitors. This issue has particularly exercized philosophers of science, most of whom have been concerned to validate the rationality of the scientific decision-making process. But for historians of science of the 1960's and since, Kuhn's critique of the notion of scientific advance was part of a much broader move away from what came to be seen as an anachronistic, "presentist" historical perspective towards one which viewed earlier science in terms of the methodological norms, metaphysics, and general cultural context of its own epoch. This move had long anticipated Kuhn; indeed he himself acknowledged the influence upon him of some of the great pioneers such as Alexander Koyré, Hélène Metzger and Anneliese Maier. One result of this move to embed science in its contemporary historical context was that historians came to consider seriously the role of extra-scientific factors--and indeed, factors which would normally be considered to be scientifically regressive or even anti-scientific--on the genesis and development of earlier science. The work of the medical historian Walter Pagel on the science of William Harvey and even more strikingly, of Frances Yates on Renaissance Hermeticism come to mind in this regard. As part of their turning away from historical presentism, historians of science have also been studying the "disreputable" pseudo-sciences and scientific traditions for their own sake, as recent studies on 16th and 17th century alchemy and on 19th century mesmerism and phrenology bear witness. The very nature of this volume, in which continuity rather than disjunction between successful and still problematic unconventionalities is highlighted, is reflective of this last point.

If our hope originally had been to produce a synoptic synthesis of how unconventionality is received by a scientific community, it will be clear (as it became clear to this writer) that, given the rich variety of approaches to the historical analysis of scientific innovation and change, such a hope was premature and even a bit simplistic. What we have instead is a group of papers which detail not only a spectrum of unconventionalities but also illustrate, explicitly or by implication, the range of historical approaches which have been developed over the past twenty years. The extremes of this range are delineated by Forman and Frankel in their papers. Forman adapts a radical "externalist" socio-cultural approach to the question of how Heisenberg's acausal physics was received in the first few years after its enunciation and publication. This paper is a sequel to an earlier study of the genesis of acausal physics in which Forman considered factors in Weimar Germany's society and culture which, he contended, preconditioned many German physicists towards a position of openness and even sympathy for a breakdown of traditional canons of causality. In the paper in this volume, Forman, as it were, tests his earlier hypothesis by comparing the responses of the British and German physicists to Heisenberg's acausal physics (his contention being that the predispositional factors at work in Germany in the 1920's were absent or present in a reduced degree in Britain).

A very different and, in a sense, complementary approach to the question of how unconventional science is received is employed by Henry R. Frankel in the next paper, "The Reception and Acceptance of Continental Drift Theory as a Rational Episode in the History of Science." Basing his approach on the model for scientific change set forth in <u>Progress and Its Problems</u> by Larry Laudan[4]--itself in part a critical response to and emendation of Kuhn in the direction of a rational, "problem-solving" model--Frankel uses an exclusively "internalist" approach and avoids entirely the issue of socio-cultural factors. Following Laudan, Frankel outlines a scheme of analysis in which competitive theories are to be evaluated on their abilities to solve research problems (those adequately solved by all rival theories), handle "anomalous" problems (those solved by one or some but not all competitors), and at the same time avoid generating serious conceptual difficulties vis-a-vis theories of related sciences and the prevalent metaphysical assumptions about modes of causality, etc.

The original theory of continental drift as proposed by Alfred Wegener did generate conceptual difficulties over the question of a mechanism for how this geological process might work. These were of such severity to render nugatory any explanatory advantages it might have had over competitive geological approaches with the result that Wegener's theory proved to be unacceptable to the geological community. But comprehensive modifications were made to continental drift theory by Wegener's successors so that by the 1960's a version had appeared with a reasonable mechanism and this won acceptance fairly rapidly, though in Frankel's view, not so speedily as one might have been led to expect on the basis of Laudan's thoroughly rationalistic model of scientific choice.

The first two papers deal with unconventionalities which have become accepted elements of their respective science; this is, at best, only partially true of the subjects of the third and fourth papers: acupuncture and parapsychology. Part of the difficulties of acupuncture, the subject of Dr. John Z. Bowers' paper, stem from a feature not present in the other cases under study in this volume and perhaps unique in the history of modern science: acupuncture is an importation from a non-western medical scientific tradition. In his paper, Dr. Bowers traces the transformation of attitudes towards acupuncture from disdain and dismissal on the part of the westernized Chinese and Japanese medical establishments and ignorance by all but a handful of western physicians to an official revival of its status under the Communist Chinese regime and a subsequent uptake of interest among western medical scientists. One important component of the reception of acupuncture was the acceptance by at least some prominent medical scientists that there actually <u>were</u> phenomena to study. Once this was granted, the next stage of the scientific "acculturation" of acupuncture could commence: its provision with a <u>modus operandi</u> familiar and acceptable to western medical scientists. This stage is still very much in progress and by no means certain in its outcome. Dr. Bowers devotes much of his paper to an account of some very recent attempts to provide a mechanism or some other acceptable explanation for acupuncture-produced phenomena.

In relation to the explanatory approaches of
Forman and Frankel, Bowers' paper (as well as that
of Mauskopf and McVaugh) falls in an intermediate
position, utilizing, implicitly, both external and
internal factors to account for acupuncture's reception. The external factors would include the
official patronage of acupuncture by the Chinese
Communist government and the development of broader and more amicable relations between Communist
China and the West, to explain how and why some
western physicians were led to examine acupuncture
seriously in the first place instead of relegating
it to the status of "pre-scientific" (and non-
western) superstition and charlatanry. The internal factors center around the clinical and neurobiological examinations of acupuncture to explain
how it works in successful cases. It might be
noted that the validation of reputed acupuncture-
derived successes is by no means easy or straight-
forward and itself gets involved in complex,
difficult-to-prove (or disprove) explanatory
schemes, such as whether acupuncture owes its
anaesthetic effects to "faith" on the part of the
test subject or to interpersonal interaction between test subject and acupuncture operator.

Parapsychology remains perhaps the arche-
typical marginal field. If it is not as ve-
hemently condemned as, say, astrology, it does not
evince even the degree of toleration acupuncture
has received. Yet parapsychologists envision
theirs as a field of experimental science and have
perennially sought acceptance, status and the
social and institutional perquisites which they
consider as their due from the scientific estab-
lishment. The paper by Mauskopf and McVaugh exam-
ines an important episode in the reception of what
was historically the most important claim to experimental success of this field in America: that
which J. B. Rhine set forth in his monograph,
Extra-Sensory Perception (1934).

Unlike the other papers in this volume, this
paper does not so much detail a "reception" as it
does the "resistance" of a small group of concerned psychologists who chose to concentrate on
the statistical evaluative methods Rhine had used
in his monograph. For Rhine had not claimed to

have produced discrete, isolatable psychic "events" in his tests for telepathy and clairvoyance but rather aggregative results in runs of card-guessing tests whose level of success was in excess of "chance expectation" to a very high degree of statistical significance.  To Rhine, the extraordinary statistical significance of his successes were indeed tantamount to proof that something other than guesswork was operating the ESP test situation, but he denied that telepathy or clairvoyance could have any physical explanation in terms of known modes of energy (and hence, information) transfer and he himself eschewed the attempt to develop a theory for psychic abilities and phenomena.

The psychologists who were first to take up the ESP issue were unable or unwilling to accept Rhine's claims and they attempted to undercut these claims by showing that Rhine's evaluation of his results as being very significant statistically was simply an artefact of his misuse of statistical methods.  Rhine, for his part, was able to enlist the aid of a number of distinguished mathematicians and statisticians in his own behalf.  By the close of 1937, the battle--or rather, the first major encounter--had been joined and essentially won by the parapsychologists and their allies.  But this victory proved to be indecisive; new charges, this time about the experimental methods as well as statistics, were raised and have proved to be very difficult to answer effectively to this day.

As has already been indicated, the paper on parapsychology, like the one on acupuncture, lends itself to a combination of both external and internal explanatory factors.  Although the controversy itself was ostensibly a technical one over statistical methods, the motivation of each group of protagonists was influenced by factors external to the statistical issues themselves.  The attacking psychologists seem  to have been negative or hostile to parapsychology to begin with and in this, to have reflected a long-standing animus to the subject on the part of the community American psychologists, and to have seized upon statistical method as the critical point of attack.  The mathematicians and statisticians who came to Rhine's defence perceived the whole issue very

differently:  fascinated by the problems in statistics raised by Rhine's work, they were either
unconcerned with or benignly disposed to parapsychology; moreover, they were stung into action
partly in response to the focus of the psychologists' attack on Rhine's statistics.  This they
perceived both as wrong-headed in itself and a
real threat to the none-too-firm status of
academic statistics in the late 1930's.

Although we have tried to consider these
four cases as a group, it is clear that the last
two differ from the first two in an obvious and
very important way:  we do not yet know the out-
comes of their attempts to gain acceptance in
mainstream science.  Indeed, there are those who
would deny that the term "science" (unconventional
or not) can properly be applied to them.  While
recognizing the real and important differences
between them and other sciences and while personally unable to predict the likelihood of their
future acceptance, I would appeal to recent
historiography of science as outlined at the beginning of this essay as justifying and even
impelling historians of science and medicine to
take seriously the history of even such marginal
fields as these--to study their histories as
analytically and dispassionately as possible.

I would like to thank our distinguished
contributors for their illuminating papers; the
AAAS for sponsoring the organization of the
original symposium and the publication of this
volume; and Mrs. Dorothy Sapp of the Department
of History, Duke University, for her admirable
handling of the typing and collation of the
manuscript.

## References

[1] 1st ed. Chicago: University of Chicago Press, 1962, 2nd. ed., 1970.

[2] Cf. Frederick Suppe (ed.), The Structure of Scientific Theories, 2nd ed. (Urbana: University of Illinois Press, 1977).

[3] Cf. Robert K. Merton and Jerry Gaston (eds.), The Sociology of Science in Europe (Carbondale: Southern Illinois University Press, 1977), especially Merton's own lead essay, "The Sociology of Science: An Episodic Memoir," 3-141.

[4] Berkeley: University of California Press, 1977.

# 1

# The Reception of an Acausal Quantum Mechanics in Germany and Britain

Paul Forman

In considering the reception of a scientific innovation, whether unconventional or otherwise, it is useful to distinguish--as Aristotle would surely have--three phases: short term, midterm, and long term. I will not attempt to characterize any of these phases except the first, for my discussion of the response to the advent of an acausal quantum mechanics will be limited to the short term--and that, moreover, only in Central Europe and the British Isles. In this initial phase, extending roughly two years, from the autumn of 1925 to the autumn of 1927, responses were, as I will argue, conditioned largely by prior expectations, predilections, and prejudices. This, however tautologously, I take as the defining characteristic of the immediate reception of innovations: people, and physicists, not only tend to find what they are looking for, but also fail to recognize what they are not prepared to see. Thus it is necessary to examine the period prior to the introduction of quantum mechanics quite as closely as that immediately following the event.

The issue, or unconventionality, to be examined is "the abandonment of causality" in the description of atomic processes. Causality, for the early twentieth century physicist, meant complete lawfulness of Nature, determinism. Unrealizable in practice, it was nonetheless regarded as the ideal goal of the science, and an assumption essential to its pursuit. While many macroscopic laws were even then being recognized as merely statistical regularities--notably the

second law of thermodynamics--it was always
supposed that the underlying microscopic events
were completely deterministic.[1]  The quantum
mechanics of atomic structure and processes introduced by Heisenberg and Schrödinger in 1925/26
proved, on the contrary, to be a self-consistent
formalism giving descriptions apparently adequate
to the test of experiment, yet providing in general not deterministic, but only probablistic
predictions about the state or behavior of these
most fundamental physical entities.[2]

The reception accorded these unquestionable
advances in the description of these basic processes was, as I will evidence, just what one
would anticipate from the antecedants.  Among
German-speaking Central-European physicists
(including, in particular, the originators of the
theory) there was immediate recognition of, and
assumption of a posture toward, the acausal
aspect of the theory and its world-view implica-
tions--corresponding to the "violent dispute over
the significance of the law of causality" which
had been raging in Germany for some years.[3]
Meanwhile, in Britain  there was nearly complete
obliviousness to the epistemic issue exercising
the Central Europeans--precisely because causality
had not in the previous years been an issue for
the British physicists.

### Germany

In a study published some years ago I described the intellectual environment in Germany
in the years immediately following her defeat
in the First World War and connected the tone and
content of that intellectual environment with the
avowed desire among a considerable segment of the
German-speaking Central-European theoretical physicists for a revolution of their science which
would eliminate "causality" from its explanatory
framework.[4]  In order now to connect the reception
of an acausal quantum mechanics with its origins,
and provide a foil to the British, it is necessary
for me to summarize parts of that study.

### The Intellectual Environment

Prior to and during the First World War
German physicists had viewed their science, if not

themselves, as closely allied with, and essential to, Germany's technically advanced industry, and with the economic and military power which that industry ensured. Confident of their value in the eyes of the public, they were self-assured, even arrogant, vis-à-vis their colleagues in the humanities and social sciences. Then, however, Germany's completely unexpected military and industrial collapse at the end of 1918 brought an immediate and extreme public reaction against the industrial-scientific idols.

This wave of anti-technologic Lebensphilosophie was a celebration of "life," intuition, unmediated and unanalyzed experience; it was a rejection of reason and logical analysis because allegedly inseparable from positivism-mechanism-materialism and because, as fundamentally disintegrative, unsatisfying of the "hunger for wholeness." Naturally, spiritualism and astrology were among its vulgar expressions. The pervasive "life" rhetoric notwithstanding, the mood of this period was distinctly pessimistic. The most popular work of Lebensphilosophie was Oswald Spengler's Untergang des Abendlandes, in which, along with forecasts of the decline of Western civilization, many pages were spent proving that even mathematics and physics were completely culture-bound and must therefore share the general fate. In the vocabulary of Lebensphilosophie there were two characteristic words: one--Anschaulichkeit, intuitiveness--had strongly positive connotations; the other--Kausalität, causality--was emphatically pejorative. And the epitome of the abstract, unintuitive, and causal mode of apprehending reality was that of the theoretical physicist. Thus, overnight, the physicists and the mathematicians--but especially the theoretical physicists--found themselves in a thoroughly hostile intellectual environment.

## Adaptations to the Environment

How did German physicists and mathematicians respond to this circumstance? At the ideological level--i.e., in their professed justifications of scientific activity, their epistemologic stance, and, generally, in their élan, their esprit, their confidence in the future of their science-- there was an astonishingly fast, far-reaching,

and unanimous adaptation to the Zeitgeist, to the
lebensphilosophisch milieu, including an espousal
of Spenglerian pessimism.  The adaptive efforts
did not stop at the ideological level.  For as
there is no clear separation between mood, motivation, and metaphysics on the one hand, and scientific activity and opinion on the other, very
soon broad movements developed in mathematics
and in theoretical physics to reconstruct the
foundations of these disciplines.  In mathematics
this was "intuitionism," a doctrine first proposed by L. E. J. Brouwer a dozen years earlier,
but which seized the Germans only now in their
altered milieu.  In theoretical physics this was,
inevitably, the renunciation of "causality."

In the seven years between the end of the
First World War and the appearance of Heisenberg's
acausal matrix mechanics, an impressive group of
German--including Austrian-German--physicists
published proposals, arguments, or exhortations
for the abandonment of causality in their science.
The list, in temporal order, includes Franz Exner,
Hermann Weyl, Richard von Mises, Walter Schottky,
Walther Nernst, Erwin Schrödinger, Arnold Sommerfeld, Hans Albrecht Senftleben, and Hans Reichen-
bach.  I have not listed the Dane Niels Bohr,
who joined this movement and necessarily had a
strong influence within it, nor have I listed
other physicists--in particular, Max Born--who
have left us indications in private papers that
they too were strongly inclined to abandon causality.  In order to establish certain essential
connections, and the non-existence of others, I
will say a few words about Weyl and about von
Mises.

Hermann Weyl, in his early thirties when
the war ended, was recognized as one of the
broadest and most talented mathematicians of his
generation.  At Göttingen circa 1910, Weyl had
been on the fringes of, and had drawn his wife
from, the circle of enthusiastic disciples around
Edmund Husserl.  In the postwar period Husserl's
doctrine of pure phenomenology degenerated into
the existentialism of Heidegger and others--i.e.,
into one of the more esoteric of the various
systems of Lebensphilosophie.  The first explicit
intrusion of Weyl's philosophic proclivities into
his scientific work was an attempt, begun in 1917,

to put the continuum of real numbers on an intui-
tionist foundation. After the war Weyl became the
principal champion in Germany of Brouwerian intuitionism. But it was not merely the ontologic and
methodologic basis of <u>mathematics</u> which Weyl felt
to be in urgent need of reform. Drawn by the
theory of relativity to theoretical physics, Weyl
was among the first to come out against causality.

Weyl came to this revolutionary position
within a year of the Armistice--in opposition
not only to his own views and scientific efforts
prior to 1918, but also as he supposed, to the
unanimous view of his colleagues. He was moved
to repudiate causality not as the result of any
scientific problems, but because the character of
the fundamental physical theories was incompatible
with the subjective, intuitive, and "for our entire experience fundamental, unidirectionality of
time"--a basic tenet of existentialism. The
solution which Weyl found was to reerect the
classical theories on an intuitionistically con-
ceived continuum. Thus, "the rigid pressure of
natural causality relaxes, and there remains,
without prejudice to the validity of natural
laws, <u>room for autonomous decisions, causally</u>
<u>absolutely independent of one another</u>, whose locus
I consider to be the elementary quanta of matter.
These 'decisions' are what is <u>actually real</u> in the
world."[5]

How is this indeterminism compatible with
the validity of natural laws, and in particular
with that thorough-going determinism which characterizes Einstein's theory of gravitation, and
Weyl's own extension of it to include electricity?
The answer lies in the analytic character which
Weyl at first attributed to physics as a whole:

> Physics . . . does not deal at all with
> the materiality, the contentness, of
> reality; rather, what it recognizes is
> solely the <u>formal constitution</u> of
> reality. It has for reality the same
> significance as formal logic for the
> realm of truth.[6]

Soon, however, Weyl restricted this characterization to the laws of classical field theory, to
gravity and electricity, thus allowing that now,

with quanta and atomicity, physics was finally in touch with the substance of reality--an acausal reality, if Nature followed Weyl's way.

The quanta which Weyl spoke of in his first manifesto, published in the spring of 1920, are simply elementary particles of matter; only some months later did Weyl invoke the quanta of action (or energy) of the quantum theory as compelling him to say "clearly and distinctly that physics in its present state is simply no longer capable of supporting the belief in a closed causality of material nature resting upon rigorously exact laws."[7]  Thus it is perfectly clear that the quantum theory was for Weyl a post factum rationalization for a position whose adoption represented an actualization of his own intellectual/ emotional proclivities by contact with a Zeitgeist of the corresponding character.

Richard von Mises, a few years older than Weyl, was one of the leading applied mathematicians of Weimar Germany.  Son of a high-ranking Jewish civil servant of the Austro-Hungarian Empire, his conservative nationalism was reinforced by the experience of being expelled by the French from Strassbourg early in 1919--along with all the other German professors at the University. His political leanings notwithstanding, von Mises, like Weyl, was attuned to contemporary philosophic, literary and artistic movements.  Between the spring of 1920 and the autumn of 1921 he converted to an explicitly Spenglerian pessimism about the future of science, repudiating not merely causality, but "the entire scheme of 'physical explanation.'"[8]  Although von Mises cited the quantum theory--i.e., the admittedly incomplete and often erroneous theory employed before the Heisenberg-Schrödinger quantum mechanics--as calling for such a thorough reconstruction, he made a point of stressing, in a paper read to his physicist colleagues, that the same conclusion must be drawn from his own field of classical mechanics, properly considered.[9]

These cases, the conversions of Weyl and von Mises, establish the influence of Lebensphilosophie in general, and of Spengler in particular. They show that considerations extrinsic to atomic physics had already predisposed some physicists to

look for--indeed long for--a quantum mechanics
cancelling causality.

## Disciplining the Renegades

The social incentives for the production of
anti-causal manifestos were so great that there
would surely have been many more published by
German theoretical physicists were there not
disciplinary forces inhibiting such apostasy.
"Apostasy" is indeed the appropriate word, for in
the absence of any clear conception of how inde-
terminacy could be combined with lawfulness, a
repudiation of causality was inevitably a repudiation of the scientific enterprise.  And indeed,
if a manifesto was to echo the prevailing pessimism, and give promise of a reform of physics
in line with the prevailing anti-rationalism,
the penitent physicist had necessarily to renounce
the traditional epistemic ambitions of his science.

The multiplication of such manifestos was
restrained by the disapprobation of some of the
older, authoritative figures in the field.  Undoubtedly often in private, and occasionally even
in public, they reasserted the indispensibility
of causality and chastised those colleagues who
so rashly and wantonly abandoned it.  The most
censurious was Wilhelm Wien, professor of experimental physics at the University of Munich, who,
although extremely flexible in adapting other
tenets to the Zeitgeist, drew the line at causality.  The most consistent and outspoken in his
adherence to causality was Max Planck, professor
of theoretical physics at the University of Berlin.
By his side stood Albert Einstein, who, while
avoiding counter-manifestos, seldom lost an opportunity to state publicly as well as privately his
antipathy to any departure from strict causality.
The third principal theoretical physicist in
Berlin, Max von Laue was undoubtedly in accord
with his two confreres.  Elsewhere, too, the
frowns of senior and influential colleagues--
and experimentalists were generally senior to
theorists--must have restrained many an impulse
to the expression of anti-causalist inclinations.

## Seizing Upon the New Theory

This then was the situation in Germany into

which Werner Heisenberg launched in the summer of
1925 a new quantum mechanics.  Heisenberg, age
24, a student of Sommerfeld, Born, and Bohr--all
anti-causalists to a lesser or greater degree--
was himself a product of the German youth movement,
which exuded Lebensphilosophie.  The acausal
character of Heisenberg's "Quantum-theoretical
Reinterpretation of Kinematic and Mechanical Relationships" was implicit in his approach.[10]  Re-
nouncing the goal of picturing the inner workings
of the atom, Heisenberg proposed as descriptive
variables new mathematical entities--infinite
matrices, as it soon appeared.  Although in
general the physical interpretation of these quantum mechanical variables was not immediately clear,
the first which Heisenberg set up, and from which
all the others were then constructed, was essentially and intentionally a table of probabilities,
namely those for the atom to make a transition
between any two of its discrete energy levels.

Heisenberg had been shuttling back and forth
along the Göttingen-Copenhagen axis during the
previous year.  His work and views were closely
related to those of Niels Bohr and Max Born, his
mentors at these termini, and to those of Wolfgang
Pauli whom he would visit in Hamburg en route.
Quickly accepted and further developed at Göttingen, the matrix mechanics was, by the end of 1925,
recognized as an important advance throughout the
German-speaking Central-European physics community,
and abroad where there was good rapport with this
geographical-cultural center of theoretical atomic
physics--notably, Leiden, Cambridge-Engl., Cam-
bridge-Mass., Pasadena.

The Unanschaulichkeit, the unintuitiveness,
and the implicit acausality of the matrix mechanics were repugnant to the conservative faction in
the German physics community.  As Erwin Schrödinger said early in 1926 in putting forward an
alternative, a continuous, causal, wave mechanics:
"we really cannot change the forms of thought,
and what cannot be understood within them cannot
be understood at all.  There are such things--but
I do not believe the structure of the atom is one
of them."[11]  Schrödinger, in his quantum mechanics
of the hydrogen atom, identified the electron with
the wave-like solution of a differential equation
of familiar form.  And, as we would expect, it was

authority.

## Britain

I have contended that the reception of an
acausal quantum mechanics by German physicists
can be understood as the continuation of a long-
standing controversy about the desired, or anticipated, character of the still-to-be-discovered
theory of atomic processes.  This controversy,
extending from the early 1920s into the years
immediately following the introduction of matrix
and wave mechanics, owed its existence to a Zeitgeist at once anti-causal and anti-scientific.
Although the point at issue was the concept of
causality, the controversy was, basically, one
between those physicists seeking to place their
science in the service of, and those wishing to
keep it insulated from, their wider intellectual
milieu.  Crucial in linking physicists and Zeitgeist, the source of the pressure to adapt, was,
I have argued, the negative valuation of abstract
physical science among the educated public at
large.  Yet, however well these theses may explain
and integrate the facts of the German case, their
validity as a general mechanism can only be tested
by cross-cultural comparisons.  I therefore offer
in the following pages a description and analysis
of the situation in Britain.  My characterizations
I think essentially correct, even though they
result from only superficial investigations.


## Science and Reason

In striking contrast with Germany, the intellectual mood in immediate post-war Britain con-
tained relatively little irrationalism.  High-brow
attitudes certainly, and even middle-brow atti-
tides on the whole, remained far from the anti-
intellectualism of the continent.  Not a trace of
it was to be found in R. B. Haldane's extremely
popular Reign of Relativity, first published in
1921.[27]  Viscount Haldane, learned statesman in
the service of higher learning, began his philo-
sophical-historical treatise with a characterization of the contemporary intellectual temper.  This
he saw as critical and anti-authoritarian; he
neither spoke irrationalism himself, nor did he
hear or see irrationalism about him.  The war

experience had, manifestly, increased his own
faith in science as a practical and ethical disci-
pline, and his general commitment to "conclusions
based on reasoned knowledge."[28]  Although in
Britain, as in Germany, fortune-telling was extremely popular among those facing the uncertain-
ties of post-war life, it was only the late 1920s
which saw in Britain a reaction of popular philosophers against "barren intellectualism," a turn
toward eastern mysticism and the "intuitive
approach."[29]

Again, in contrast with the Germans' reaction against physical science as a god that failed,
there is every indication that the prestige of
science was extremely high in Britain--higher than
before the war, higher than was pleasing to some
contemporary culture-critics.  "Science had gradually become the faith of numerous cold-blooded
people who had no use for revealed religion . . ."
Robert Graves observed from a distance of two
decades, thus confirming, but with a different
valuation, Haldane's characterization.[30]  The
attention to, and support of, applied science,
begun during the war, continued in the post-war
period without any such ideological break as
occurred in Germany.[31]  In all anticipations of
the future, whether optimistic or pessimistic,
natural science and its technical applications
were accorded a very large role.[32]  "Epoch-making"
discoveries of a thoroughly practical sort were
standard newspaper fare,[33] and the demand for
popular expositions of the results of fundamental
physical research--and not merely of relativity--
was very high.  In 1926 a reviewer for Nature
observed that:

> Whatever  properties may ultimately be
> assigned to the atom, there is one which
> cannot be omitted--its power to seize and
> captivate the human mind.  In fact, if we
> judged by the output of the printing press
> in the last few years, we might not un-
> fairly assume that no sooner does any one
> fall within the sphere of influence of
> this radiating personality than he is
> seized with an irresistible determination
> to go home and write a book about it.
> Nor is the proselytising zeal confined to
> the pure physicist, whose protegé the

the atom may be presumed to be. We
have books on the atom, some of them
quite well done, by chemists, by mathematicians, by technicians, and by journal-
ists, and addressed to all sorts and
conditions of readers. Thus we have
"Atoms for Amateurs," "Atoms for Adepts,"
"Atoms for Adolescents," "Atoms for
Archdeacons," "All about Atoms for Any-
body"--these are not the exact titles,
but they indicate the scope of the
volumes well enough--in fact, there seems
to be a determination that no class of
reader shall be left without an exposition of the subject suited to his condi-
tion and attainments. As these volumes
continue to pour forth--there are two
fresh ones before us as we write--we must
assume that they find purchasers and
readers. If we add to these the enormous
output of serious scientific contributions
from the many laboratories engaged in
investigating the structure and properties of the atom, it is clear that this
infinitesimal particle exerts an attrac-
tion unique in the history of science
over the minds and imaginations of many
types of men.[34]

Such popular expositions were indeed bought.
In 1929 the entire printing of James Jeans' Universe Around Us, 7500 copies, was sold out in one
month. The following year the initial printing,
10,000 copies, of his Mysterious Universe was
sold on the day of publication, and the book continued to sell as fast as it could be printed and
bound: 1000 copies a day for a month.[35]

Far from continuing to decline in stature
in the eyes of artists and literary intellectuals,
physicists seem to have gained a measure of respect which they had long ceased to expect from
that quarter. To be sure, in the first three
decades of the century literary circles were less
anti-intellectualist in Britain than on the continent. A Bertrand Russell, a Maynard Keynes, a
Julian Huxley could be at home in Bloomsbury or
in the group surrounding Lady Ottoline Morrell.
It was rather D. H. Lawrence, with his deep anger
at science, and his belief in the power of "the

dark loins of man," who was regarded in such company as <u>outré</u>. And in this respect there seems to have been no significant difference between the wartime and the early postwar years.[36] Against the limited following Lawrence gained, one must place J. W. N. Sullivan's testimony (1927) that "there can be no doubt that the prestige of science has greatly increased in recent times." Before the war the view of Nietzsche, Dostoievsky, and Tolstoi,

> that the man of science was not a human being . . . became very popular with artists of all kinds. . . . It is evident that the position today is rather different. It has become different since the war. . . . The change was, I believe, due to Einstein . . . the respect of imaginative people for science in general has greatly increased . . . the result appears to have been disastrous. At a time when the physicists are abandoning materialism, the artists are accepting it.[37]

Given these circumstances, the morale of the British physicists ought to have been high. And so it appears to have been. In March 1924, welcoming their distinguished guests, including the Duke of York and Prime Minister Ramsey MacDonald, to the celebration of the fiftieth anniversary of the Physical Society of London, F. E. Smith gave it voice: "Gentlemen, we are not only proud of the past, but confident of the future," etc., etc.[38] It is impossible to imagine the corresponding German association, the Deutsche Physikalische Gesellschaft, entertaining guests of equivalent rank in German society and government. Moreover, should it, impossibly, have had the opportunity to do so, it is impossible to imagine its spokesman so unqualifiedly confident. Thus, according to the model I have advanced to link the physicists' ideology and conceptual predilections to the <u>Zeitgeist</u>, the British, in contrast with the Germans, should have felt little inclination to alter the one or the other in any radical or revolutionary way.

## Mind Over Matter

But <u>were</u> there any predilections of the

British mind of this period which were contrary
to the established goals, methods, or world-
picture of the science of physics?  If by "mind"
we understand the highbrow synoptic-synthetic
thinkers, the answer is, curiously, "yes."   R. B.
Haldane summed it up fairly well as a repudiation
of the Victorian scientist's bifurcation of the
world into an objective reality of matter and
motion and a subjective world of qualities and
values which are merely mental.  On the contrary,
for Haldane and most of the other British philosophers, the world

> exhibits mechanistic features, but it also
> has biological aspects not less important.
> It discloses the shaping influences of
> ends, and it possesses colour and beauty
> and value . . . there is a single whole
> within which fall matter and mind alike.
> . . . such is at least the view which is
> beginning to be insisted on in the twen-
> tieth century, even in scientific circles.[39]

A virtual litany of like convictions and anticipations fills the two volumes of personal credos
published in 1924 and 1925 as Contemporary British
Philosophy.  In most cases they are expressions of
a comprehensive panpsychism or hylozoism.[40]

The rise of analytic philosophy--and the
concomitant  resignation of the philosopher's
grand pretensions--has so colored our perspective
that it is difficult to recognize the situation as
it was in the early 1920s: the established philosophers were still overwhelmingly metaphysical
idealists, who, straight out, "define philosophy
as the systematic study of the ultimate nature of
reality," and who declare that ultimate reality
to be mind.[41]  Although hindsight enforces the
qualification "still . . . metaphysical idealists,"
in fact these men seem not to have yet had an
inkling of their fate.  Nothing could have aston-
ished them more than to learn how completely they,
and their endeavours, have disappeared from the
philosophers' history.[42]  For as Haldane suggests,
they were convinced that history was on their side.
Above all, the recent development of physical
science (Relativity!) seemed to many of them evidence of this sea change, for which in the early
1920s A. N. Whitehead came to be the most

applauded, though perhaps least radical, theorist.[43]

This characteristic anticipation of, or
program for, the transformation of science may be
seen as the British version of the revolution in
Wissenschaft which Fritz Ringer showed to be so
urgently desired by German humanists and social
scientists in the decades after 1890.[44]  Both
originated as a reaction against scientific
naturalism, but equally as a reaction against the
relative decline in "relevance" and cultural influence of the humanistic scholar in the indus-
trialized mass societies emerging in both countries in the late nineteenth century.

Yet while "Kausalität" became the principal
target of the German ideologist, "causality" seems
to have come only slowly, lately, and uncertainly
within the sights of the British.  Panpsychism,
for example, may be elected to facilitate an
alteration of the course of nature by mind, and
thus provide an escape from physical determinism.
It may also, following Spinoza, with equal logic
provide the basis for a thorough-going determinism,
psychical as well as physical.  In fact, the
British idealist philosophers of the period appear
to have been divided roughly equally between
acausalists and causalists.[45]  More to the point,
recent developments in physics were not seen as
bearing upon this issue.  Although on the whole
British philosophers paid much more attention, and
gave much greater weight, to the results of scientific research than did their opposite numbers in
Germany, and although most were concerned to
bridge the gap between the mental and physical
worlds, and although many sought to exclude mechanical causation from the organic world, nonetheless in the early 1920s not one British philosopher,
so far as I am aware, drew from contemporary physics ammunition for an assault upon causality.[46]

This is the more surprising as there are
indeed some indications of a gradual increase in
Britain, between 1919 and 1925, of preoccupation
with, and antipathy toward, causality.  Haldane,
for example, uses the word completely unselfcon-
sciously and unpejoratively in The Reign of Relativity (1921), but not so in his contribution to
Contemporary British Philosophy (1924).  The most

striking document in this connection is the collection of essays, Science, Religion and Reality
(1925), edited by Joseph Needham. Here a series
of scholars, some older and distinguished, some
younger and soon to be distinguished, each drawing
upon his own special field, unencumbered by
scholarly apparatus, but respectful of their
readers, gave their individual perspectives on the
relation of Wissenschaft to religion and an ultimate reality.[47]

The collection was profiled by Arthur James
Balfour, our second example of that uniquely
British phenomenon, the statesman metaphysician.
The essence of the conflict between science and
religion lay, according to Lord Balfour, not in
the factual but in the emotional sphere, in the
character of the contemporary physical world
picture: "the very lucidity of the new conceptions
helps to bring home to us their essential insuffi-
ciency as a theory of the universe. . . . No man
really supposes that he personally is nothing more
than a changing group of electrical charges." His
plea for free will, for recognition that human
action "constitutes spiritual invasion of the
physical world," was certainly a volte-face for
the Chancellor of Cambridge University. Yet
Balfour still vacillated on the issue of physical
determinism, using the word "causality" now pe-
joratively, now unpejoratively, finding the diver-
gence between prediction and observation of the
flow of physical events now necessary and intrinsic, now merely "because our knowledge of natural
processes is small, and our power of calculation
feeble."[48]

Needham himself came forward here with that
combination of metaphysical panpsychism and
physical mechanism which he reiterated so often in
the following years.[49] And Charles Singer, although giving indeterminists no encouragement,
concluded his survey of the historical conflicts
between science and religion by recognizing that
"the tyranny of determinism" was an urgent problem
for some scientists too.[50] One such was yet
another contributor to this collection, who, however, declined to accept the traditional refuge,
i.e. the Spinozist combination of panpsychism and
determinism. But let us defer for a few pages the
unique case of Arthur Stanley Eddington.

Summing up our view of the intellectual environment for the science of physics in post-war
Britain: here, as in Germany, the deterministic
world-picture of the physicists had some high-brow
opposition reaching back a full generation, and
increasing in intensity in the period considered.
But in Britain, in contrast with Germany, the irrationalism which put steam into the issue of causality, was never quite acceptable in high-brow
circles, and became popular at middle-brow only
in the late 1920s.  Further, whatever may have
been the causes of the manifestations of anti-
determinism among British synoptic-synthetic
thinkers in the years following the First World
War, the general lack of focus of this sentiment--
as indicated, _inter alia_, by the absence of any
anti-shibboleth corresponding to "Kausalität"--and
the continued strongly positive valuation of
physical science, effectively neutralized the
conditions under which, on our model, any widespread or far-reaching influence upon working
physicists could be expected.  Moreover, in the
British case the anti-determinist sentiments began
to appear so late that they could scarcely have
had an impact in the period considered.  But let
us look at British physicists and see how our expectations are met.

## Before Quantum Mechanics

Outside of Cambridge, where R. H. Fowler
mediated contact with Central European work, the
British physicists were not very active partici-
pants in the problems of theoretical spectroscopy
and quantum statistics.  They had, however, been
continuously involved with problems of emission,
absorption, and dispersion of radiation, and thus
continuously puzzled by the contradiction between
the wave theory of light and its particle-like
properties.[51]

Charles G. Darwin, the great man's grandson
and a leading figure among theoretical physicists
in Britain, made several proposals, over a period
of more than a decade, for approaching these
problems by altering the classical equations of
mechanics and abandoning the conservation of energy
in atomic processes.  But of a failure of causality,
of unambiguous determination of atomic events,

there is no serious thought in his mind.[52]

Confronting the logical contradiction between continuous extension and local concentration of radiant energy, Owen Richardson, one of Britain's most able physicists from the school and in the style of J. J. Thomson, suggested "it may be that it is impossible consistently to describe the spacial distribution of radiation in terms of three-dimensional geometry."[53] This was a more radical thought, and Bohr cited it as a precursor of his own doubts "whether the detailed interpretation of the interaction between matter and radiation can be given at all in terms of a causal description in space and time of the kind hitherto used for the interpretation of natural phenomena."[54] But Richardson's suggestion certainly need not, and in his own mind almost certainly did not, imply any failure of causality.

I have mentioned Darwin and Richardson because they were recognized leaders of theoretical physics in Britain in the early 1920s and because they have been cited as anticipators of an acausal quantum mechanics[55]—which they were not. There is, however, one British physicist who was.

Norman Robert Campbell, though no more than highly capable as physicist, was surely one of the most unfettered critical minds of his generation, and among the most acute methodologists in the sciences. Early in 1926 he published under the title "Time and Chance" thoughts which had evidently been with him for some time.[56] He proposed that "time, like temperature, is a purely statistical conception, having no meaning except as applied to statistical aggregates" of atoms, "that the ultimate magnitude, the statistical average of which is a temporal magnitude, is the probability . . . of a transition," and consequently that chance must be accepted as fundamental and irreducible in the course of nature. Apparently Campbell was prompted to publish his proposal, even though confessedly unable to make a working theory of it, by the appearance of the first papers on matrix mechanics. He found Heisenberg's positivism an attractive approach to atomic dynamics, but in the theory itself he seems to have recognized no affinity with his own. Indeed, although his proposal is for a fundamentally acausal theory, he himself never even uses the words "causality" or "determinism."

Evidently, all of these Britons--Darwin, Richardson, and also Campbell--present fundamentally different cases than the German theoretical physicists authoring manifestos against causality. Not only do their doubts and their proposals differ conceptually and semantically from the Germans', but also the form, rhetoric, occasion, audience, etc. of the documents advancing them show the British to be thinking only of their fellow physicists and without concern for their public image.

But let us now turn to the case of A. S. Eddington, and first of all to the manifesto-- essentially of the same character as the more respectable of the German Bekenntnisse--which Eddington published in Science, Religion, and Reality. Although Lord Balfour, in his "Introduction," had found nothing in contemporary science to meliorate the conflict between human freedom and physical determinism, Eddington, speaking for "the Domain of Physical Science,' undertook to do just that.[57]

The core of Eddington's position, that the field theories of physics provide merely formal, logical, indeed tautological, connections between the "entities of the world," is strikingly similar to Hermann Weyl's, whose "conversion," said Eddington, "is very recent--as indeed is my own." But where existentialist Weyl had taken these entities, whose "intrinsic essence" lies outside the province of physics, to be the "autonomous decisions" localized in the elementary particles, the quanta of matter, Eddington, panpsychist and Friend, made these entities the elementary particles themselves, animated by "Mind, the Logos." The properties and behavior of the "entities of the world," the as yet undiscovered laws of atomic structure and of the quantum, "may be true laws of governance"--by which Eddington did not mean that these "transcendental" laws will be deterministic. On the contrary, because physics here, finally, makes contact with consciousness, "it may be that the normal laws are such that they can be set aside by human free will."[58]

Superadded to this already somewhat confused position are largely gratuitous elements of existentialism, in particular "actuality" as "another undoubted fact of experience which is left out of the scheme of theoretical physics," and of which account can be taken only by means of, and along with, consciousness.[59]

As with Weyl, Eddington's position in 1925 was the result of a gradual development extending back some half-dozen years. His earliest statements on the question appeared in 1920. These are so essentially connected with the character of Einstein's theory of gravity, and its generalization by Weyl, that it is difficult to imagine Eddington having come to such views much more than a year before.[60] In his initial position, admirably clear and unencumbered, there was no existentialism, no indeterminism, not even any panpsychism. It was, simply, that mind is no part of nature, views nature from outside, and constructs from the four-dimensional manifold of "point-events," which nature is postulated to be, a world whose order is mind's own. This being so it is possible, even likely, that the laws which are intrinsic to nature—those of atomicity and quanta—may prove to be "irrational."[61]

"Behavior whose laws are irrational," Eddington observed in retrospect, "was perhaps as near to the conception of undetermined behavior as the thought of the time could reach."[62] But Weyl, as we saw, in a German-speaking Central-European milieu arrived at indeterminism very quickly, and with little apparent difficulty. In the following years Weyl, whose work in relativity was the most important stimulus for Eddington's own, undoubtedly played an important role also in the development of Eddington's indeterminism and of his philosophic views generally. In particular, Weyl is the obvious source for Eddington's existentialist preoccupation with "actuality" and the unindirectionality of time, which is otherwise thoroughly uncharacteristic of British philosophy in this period.[63] Weyl is, in fact, the only person to whom Eddington refers in "The Domain of Physical Science," citing and quoting him repeatedly.

Eddington's case is similar to that of the

German acausalists in that his manifestos were not
a response to scientific difficulties but an expression of religious-philosophical yearnings.
Eddington differs, however, from most of his German
counterparts in that he, like Weyl, deserves to be
taken seriously.  He struggled continually with
these epistemic problems, and "audience reactions"
were evidently not uppermost in his mind.  His
case is unique in Britain, but he was not entirely
alone.  Indeed, it is impossible to think of
Eddington in this period, the mid-1920s, without
thinking immediately of J. H. Jeans.  Whether or
not Jeans himself had strong views on free will
and determinism--and I doubt that he did--it would
have been out of character for him not to seek to
outdo Eddington on this issue too.  Ironically,
the opportunity which he chose to tantalize an
audience with the prospect that "the deadly inevi-
tability of cause and effect has ended" was the
award of the gold medal of the Royal Astronomical
Society, early in 1926, to Albert Einstein.[64]  And
again, in President Jeans' address the only contemporary other than Einstein to be mentioned is
Hermann Weyl--both for his work in relativity and
for his suggestion that the quantum will change
the universe into "a drama in which all the actors
choose their actions as the play proceeds."  Jeans
is a puzzle; he seems not to have repeated this
performance.

Although the anti-causal inclinations of an
Eddington (or a Jeans) are most pertinent to the
principal question here addressed, they were not
characteristic for their milieu.  Far more typical
for British natural-philosophical thought in this
period is that interpretation of the conceptual
situation in physics advanced by Lancelot Law
Whyte in 1927 in Archimedes, or the Future of
Physics, namely that "in order to straighten out
its atomic problems physics will have to take a
hint from biology."[65]  This notion, casually
stated in the language of the work-a-day world,
had come to Whyte two years before as a most powerful experience, a veritable revelation.

> 3 am August 21st 1925.  An idea the impli-
> cations of which are so tremendous that
> they appal me . . . A revolution of
> thought comparable to that of Einstein
> but wider, more fertile & synthetic in its

effect.  It indeed would be the
fitting & perhaps the only fitting
crown to <u>all</u> the dreams in my being.
. . . How the stress came:--lying in
the bed--thoughts of masturbation--an
appeal to enter God's being, to dive
into the Depths of Christ . . . <u>the</u>
<u>idea</u>.  That <u>just as</u> the Solution of
<u>Relativity</u> demanded a fundamental re-
consideration of the so-called <u>limits</u>
of Science & their absorption into
Science & reconstruction & a new understanding of them, <u>So</u> the solution of
the Relativity-Quantum problem might
involve the problem of life in such a
way as to throw real light on the relation of Religion, Art & Science.[66]

Whyte soon recognized that his illumination
was not unique.  On the contrary, "the last few
years," he wrote in 1927, "constitute another
critical period," similar to that in which the idea
of evolution by natural selection emerged simultaneously in different minds,

since an idea, which when made precise
will transform scientific thought, has
already come independently to many
thinkers.  Since 1922 many scientists
have felt that in studying the emission
and absorption of light physics has come
near to the problem of life.

Here Whyte cited Whitehead, first of all, then
Eddington who "comes near to the same idea," and
thirdly, Weyl.  "It has also been expressed by
others quite independently, though I do not know
of other published references."[67]

The point particularly to be noted is that
while Whyte anticipates a revolution in science,
indeterminism receives no explicit attention, let
alone a leading role; Whyte is simply unconcerned
with that aspect of Weyl's and Eddington's views.
And this seems characteristic.  In July, 1924, the
program of the joint meeting of the Aristotelian
Society and the Mind Association included a symposium on the quantum theory, chaired by Whitehead,
with contributions by J. W. Nicholson, D. Wrinch,
F. A. Lindemann, and H. Wildon Carr.[68]  The very

title of the symposium--"The Quantum Theory: How
far does it modify the mathematical, the physical
and the psychological concepts of continuity?"--
shows how very far the British were from focusing
on causality.  Of the four speakers only Nicholson
raised the issue; after stressing the strictly
probablistic character of the current theory, he
ascribed that characteristic to its incomplete-
ness.[69]

## After Quantum Mechanics

        What then happened, how did the British phy-
sicists respond, when, in the latter half of 1925
and the first half of 1926 the papers on matrix
and wave mechanics appeared in German journals?
In particular how did they react to the intrinsi-
cally acausal character of the matrix mechanics
and to Born's acausal interpretation of the wave
mechanics?  If the hypothesis which I advanced in
discussing the reception of quantum mechanics by
German physicists is general, then here in Britain
too the reactions to quantum mechanics should be
inferrable from the positions previously taken on
the likely or desirable character of an adequate
atomic theory, and particularly from prior align-
ments respecting causality.  And if "causality"
was previously not an issue--as, by and large, it
was not in Britain?  Then we should expect that
in the near term, the first couple of years, the
British physicists would remain oblivious to the
problematic of physical interpretation and, especially, to any broader epistemic implications.

        Indeed, that is just the way it was.  Apart
from translations of expositions by Max Born and
Pascual Jordan (translations prepared, and their
publication likely instigated, by J. Robert Oppen-
heimer) there was in the pages of Nature through
1927 nothing showing any awareness of the epistemologic issues[70]--nothing except the one-paragraph
summary of Eddington's fifth Gifford lecture.  But
let's look briefly at the British physicists previously mentioned.

        In February 1927, O. W. Richardson addressed
the Physical Society of London, as its President,
on "The Present State of Atomic Physics."  Although
he gave a couple of pages to the matrix mechanics
and emphasized its mathematical equivalence to the

wave mechanics, Richardson spoke as an avowed
partisan of the latter theory: "the electron is
regarded as a train of waves."[71] That there was
anything problematic in this interpretation Richardson did not even hint. He said not a word
about probabilities.

Again, in February 1927, C. G. Darwin published an extension of the formalism of wave
mechanics to encompass the spin of the electron.
He proposed "assimilating the electron to a trans-
verse rather than a longitudinal wave." As in
his previous proposals for modifying dynamics,
Darwin was thinking about tinkering with the mathematical form of the equations--to be sure, the most
fundamental equations--but of the interpretive
issues he seems not to have had an inkling.[72]

And once again, in February 1927, R. H.
Fowler, who of all British physicists had the
closest rapport with atomic theory in Central
Europe, provided Nature with a short exposition
for the scientific public of "Matrix and Wave
Mechanics." Fowler stressed the equivalence of
these two systems of calculation, their complete-
ness and finality: "We have at last a general
dynamical method to apply to any atom, which is
capable of yielding us by direct calculation any
result for which we may ask."[73] That there were
important classes of results for which one may
not even ask--such as the position of an electron,
or the time of an atomic transition--Fowler either
failed to see, or thought unimportant to say.

Not even N. R. Campbell--I think it fair to
say--had in the spring of 1927 yet recognized the
indeterminism of the new quantum mechanics. Re-
sponding in the pages of Nature to Pascual Jordan's
provocative question, "Will it ever happen that
the time of a quantum jump is undetermined?,"
Campbell replied, "Certainly."[74] But his certainty
derived entirely from his own view that time is a
statistical concept which has meaning only for an
aggregate of atoms. He saw no such implication
in the new quantum mechanics, and to the end of the
year seems to have remained cool, if not uncompre-
hending, toward Heisenberg's uncertainty principle.[75]

There was, however, as I indicated, one exception to this general obliviousness toward the

epistemic bearing of the new quantum mechanics.  In
the first months of 1927 Eddington was delivering
at the University of Edinburgh the prestigious
Gifford Lectures, which obliged him to relate his
science to broader questions of philosophy and religion.[76]  The fifth of these Eddington devoted to
atomic physics and its bearing upon free will, de-
claring that, as a result of the new quantum mechanics, "all the determinism is removed from the
laws of physics . . . whatever view we may take of
free will on philosophical grounds, we cannot
appeal to physics against it."[77]  In recognizing
and seizing upon the acausal character of the new
theories Eddington is highly exceptional--probably
unique--among British physicists.  Relative, however, to our model for receptivity, Eddington is
no exception, but rather confirms our expectations.[78]

     In the middle term and long term the British
gradually came around.  (Eddington found the process infuriatingly slow.[79])  The Solvay Congress
of October 1927 was an important educational
experience which opened the eyes of the partici-
pating British physicists to the inescapably
acausal character of the quantum mechanics.[80]
They strongly favored the wave mechanics because
the mathematics was familiar and the atomic processes were rendered in some sense pictorially.
The statistical character of the wave function
was unwelcome, but gradually accepted.[81]

     In the examining the reception of an acausal
quantum mechanics I have dealt exclusively with
the near term, the first two years, and I have
described the attitudes and preoccupations, established in the preceding years, with which the
physicists met this innovation.  I argued that
only in Germany was the indeterminism of the
theory immediately recognized and seized upon by
significant number of physicists, and that that
was an expression of their wish to achieve for
their science a more favorable regard by the
public.  In Britain, by contrast, where the intellectual environment placed the physicists under
no pressure and causality had not previously been
a clear and important issue, the epistemic bearing
of the new theory was simply overlooked, and the
more congenial of its formalisms was adopted un-
critically.

## References

[1] Stephen G. Brush, The Kind of Motion We Call Heat: A History of the Kinetic Theory of Gases in the 19th Century, 2 vols. (Amsterdam, 1976), and "Irreversibility and Indeterminism: Fourier to Heisenberg," Jour. of the Hist. of Ideas, 1976, 37: 603-630. These publications give, respectively, general background and a qualification of my generalization.

[2] Friedrich Hund, Geschichte der Quantentheorie (Mannheim, 1967); Max Jammer, The Conceptual Development of Quantum Mechanics (New York, 1966).

[3] Quoting Max Planck, Kausalgesetz und Willensfreiheit. Öffentlicher Vortrag gehalten in der Preuss. Akad. d. Wiss. am. 17. Februar 1923 (Berlin, 1923), reprinted in Planck, Vorträge und Erinnerungen (Stuttgart, 1949), 139-168, esp. 140.

[4] P. Forman, "Weimar Culture, Causality, and Quantum Theory, 1918-1927: Adaptation by German Physicists and Mathematicians to a Hostile Intellectual Environment," Historical Studies in the Physical Sciences, 1971, 3:1-115.

[5] Weyl, "Das Verhältnis der kausalen zur statistischen Betrachtungsweise in der Physik," Schweizerische Naturforschende Gesellschaft, Verhl. (1919), Teil II, 152-153; Schweizerische Medizinische Wochenschrift, 1920, 50:737-741. Only this latter publication is reprinted in Weyl's Gesammelte Abhandlungen, 4 vols. (Berlin, 1968), 2: 113-122.

[6] Weyl, Raum, Zeit, Materie, 1st ed. (Berlin, 1918), 227.

[7] Ibid., 4th ed. (Berlin, 1921), 283-284; preface dated Nov. 1920.

[8] R. v. Mises, Naturwissenschaft und Technik der Gegenwart. Eine akademische Rede mit Zusätzen (Leipzig, 1922), 19.

[9]R. v. Mises, "Über die gegenwärtige Krise der Mechanik," Zeitschr. f. angewandte Math. u. Mech., 1921, 1:425-431, and Naturwiss, 1922, 10: 25-29.

[10]Heisenberg, "Über quantentheoretische Umdeutung kinematischer und mechanischer Beziehungen," Zeitschr. f. Phys., 1925, 33:879-893, translated in B. L. van der Waerden, ed., Sources of Quantum Mechanics (New York, 1969), which also translates the following papers of and with Max Born and Pascual Jordan developing Heisenberg's scheme into a consistent and comprehensive calculus of matrices.

[11]E. Schrödinger, "Quantisierung als Eigenwertproblem (Zweite Mitteilung)," Annalen der Physik, 1926, 79:489-527 (509). The entire series of papers was collected as Abhandlungen zur Wellenmechanik (Leipzig, 1928) and translated as Collected Papers on Wave Mechanics (London, 1928).

[12]Letters on Wave Mechanics: Schrödinger, Planck, Einstein, Lorentz, compiled by K. Przibram, trans. and introduced by Martin J. Klein (New York, 1967); Schrödinger's letters to W. Wien, 1926-27, of which copies are deposited in the Archive for History of Quantum Physics, Berkeley, Philadelphia, Copenhagen.

[13]In Britain, in particular, apart from Dirac's work and G. Birtwistle's The New Quantum Mechanics (Cambridge, 1928), the texts and applications of quantum mechanis were of the wave mechanics exclusively.

[14]Heisenberg to Jordan, München [1926] Jul. 28: "Vor ein paar Tagen hab ich hier zwei Vorträge von Schrödinger gehort und bin seitdem von der Unrichtigkeit der von Schrödinger vertretenen physikalischen Interpretation der Qu. M. felsenfest überzeugt." (Archive for History of Quantum Physics.)

[15]M. Born, "Zur Quantenmechanik der Stossvorgänge (vorläufige Mitteilung)," ZS. f. Phys., 1926, 37:863-67; "Quantenmechanik der Stossvorgänge,"

ibid., 1926, 38:803-827; "Das Adiabatenprinzip in
der Quantenmechanik," ibid., 1926, 40:167-192;
"Zur Wellenmechanik der Stossvorgänge," Ges. d.
Wissensch., Göttingen, Nachr. (1927), 146-160.
These papers are reprinted in Max Born, Zur sta-
tistischen Deutung der Quantentheorie, ed. Armin
Hermann (Stuttgart, 1962).

[16]Born, ZS. f. Phys., 37:863, received 1926
June 25, included a note apologizing to his fellow
physicists, the readership of the Zeitschrift für
Physik, for the form of this initial publication.
Born explained that the paper was intended for Die
Naturwissenschaften but lack of space prevented its
acceptance.

[17]Born, ZS. f. Phys., 38:826, received 1926
July 21.

[18]Compare, for example, the photographs of
Born and Heisenberg in Armin Hermann, Werner
Heisenberg, 1901-1976 (Bonn-Bad Godesberg: Inter
Nationes, 1976), esp. those on pages 20 and 48.

[19]See Hund, Gesch. d. Qu. Th. (1967) and
Jammer, Conceptual Dev. of Q. M. (1966).

[20]W. Heisenberg, "Über den anschaulichen
Inhalt der quantentheoretischen Kinematik und
Mechanik," ZS. f. Phys., 1927, 43:172-198, re-
ceived 1927 Mar. 23. Quotations from p. 197.

[21]". . . einfach ein logisches Versehen."
Hugo Bergmann, Der Kampf um das Kausalgesetz in
der jüngsten Physik (Braunschweig, 1929), 39.

[22]Born, loc. cit., note 17.

[23]Heisenberg, loc. cit., note 14.

[24]Heisenberg, "Quantentheoretische Mechanik,"
Deutsche Mathematiker-Vereinigung, Jahresber.,
1927, 36:24*-25*. Abstract of lecture at the
Naturforscherversammlung, Düsseldorf, 1926 Sep. 23.

[25]Heisenberg, "Quantenmechanik," Naturw.,
1926, 14:989-994.

[26]M. Born and W. Heisenberg, "La mécanique
des quanta," Electrons et photons. Rapports et
discussions due cinquième conseil de physique
[Solvay] . . . 1927 (Paris, 1928), 143-181, on
p. 144. Having achieved this "quantentheoretische
Umdeutung," so to speak, of Anschaulichkeit, Heisenberg was free to deprecate the "populäre
Anschaulichkeit" of Schrödinger's wave mechanics:
op. cit., note 20, 196.

[27]Richard Burdon, Viscount Haldane, The
Reign of Relativity (1st ed., London, 1921 May;
3rd ed., 1921 August).

[28]Haldane, 3rd ed., p. 4.

[29]Robert Graves and Alan Hodge, The Long
Week-End. A Social History of Great Britain
1918-1939 (London, 1940), 23, 202-203.

[30]Ibid., 91.

[31]Henry Frank Heath and A. L. Hetherington,
Industrial Research and Development in the United
Kingdom, a Survey (London, 1946).

[32]E.g., J. B. S. Haldane, Daedalus, or Science and the Future (London, 1923), and the reply
by Bertrand Russell, Icarus, or The Future of
Science (London, 1924).

[33]Graves and Hodge, The Long Week-End (1940),
92-93.

[34]"The Atom Again," Nature, 1926, 118:365.

[35]S. C. Roberts, "Memoir," in E. A. Milne,
Sir James Jeans. A Biography (Cambridge, 1952),
x-xi.

[36]Julian Huxley, Memories (London, 1970), 114,
160; Bertrand Russell, Autobiography, 2 vols.

(London, 1967), passim; R. F. Harrod, The Life of John Maynard Keynes (London, 1951), Chs. 5 and 6.

[37]J. W. N. Sullivan, Gallio, or The Tyranny of Science (London, 1927), 8-16. Of this negative valuation there was scarcely a hint in the collection of occasional pieces, Aspects of Science, which Sullivan published two years earlier.

[38]Physical Society, London, The Physical Society of London 1874-1924. Proceedings at the Jubilee Celebration Meetings (London, 1924), 2.

[39]Haldane, Reign of Relativity, 19.

[40]J. H. Muirhead, ed., Contemporary British Philosophy: Personal Statements (First Series) (London, 1924); . . . (Second Series) (London, 1925).

[41]J. M. E. McTaggart, ibid. (First Series), 251.

[42]E.g., the chapters on philosophy in C. B. Cox and A. E. Dyson, eds., The Twentieth-Century Mind. History, Ideas, and Literature in Britain, 3 vols. (London, 1972). G. J. Warnock, English Philosophy since 1900 (London, 1958), used his first brief chapter, "The Point of Departure," to make exactly this point, and then proceeded to give a history in which the metaphysics and idealism were completely omitted.

[43]A. N. Whitehead, The Concept of Nature (Cambridge, 1920) and numerous subsequent publications. Often assimilated to Whitehead's views were these of Samuel Alexander, whose Space, Time, and Deity, The Gifford Lectures . . . 1916-1918 (London, 1920; repr. 1927), was again highly regarded. Neither was an anti-causalist in the period or sense here treated. Haldane (Reign of Relativity, 117) quotes, and seemingly misconstrues, Whitehead's dictum that "causal nature is a metaphysical chimera" (Concept of Nature, 32). Whitehead was here speaking not against causality, but, like Husserl, against the hypostatization of

a physical world devoid of qualities which is the cause of our perceptions of qualities.

[44]Fritz K. Ringer, Decline of the German Mandarins. The German Academic Community, 1890-1933 (Cambridge, Mass., 1969).

[45]Carveth Read and C. Lloyd Morgan, for example, were panpsychists espousing a thoroughgoing determinism: Muirhead, Contemp. Brit. Phil. (First Series), 278, 352-54.

[46]The British forewent a unique opportunity, which in Germany would unquestionably have led to a colorful nosegay of anti-causal manifestos: the lectureship founded in the Scottish universities by Lord Adam Gifford to treat Natural Theology in the widest sense of the word.  As Rudolf Metz, A Hundred Years of British Philosopy (London, 1938), 779, observed, "this stimulating seed fell upon fertile soil.  The greater part of the output of speculative thought in Great Britain since 1888, when the first Gifford Lectures were given, bears the name of this magnanimous foundation."

[47]Joseph Needham, ed., Science, Religion, and Reality (London and New York, 1925), with contributions by A. J. Balfour, Bronislaw Malinowski, Charles Singer, Antonio Aliotta, A. S. Eddington, J. Needham, J. W. Oman, Wm. Brown, Clement C. J. Webb, and Wm. R. Inge.

[48]A. J. Balfour, "Introduction" to idem, pp. 1-18; quotations from pp. 15, 17, 13, 17 respectively.  Balfour had been moving ideologically very rapidly in the previous year or two.  In his recent Gifford Lectures, 1922-23, he had shown himself still sympathetic to the scientific world view and still prepared to concede "that every belief is without exception causally determined, and, in the last resort, determined by antecedents which are not beliefs, nor indeed psychical events of any kind, but belong wholly to the non-rational world of matter and motion."  Theism and Thought (London, 1923), 21.

[49]J. Needham, "Mechanist Biology and the

Religious Consciousness," in Science, Religion, and Reality (1925), 219-258; The Sceptical Biologist (New York, 1930).

[50]C. Singer, "Historical Relations of Religion and Science," in Science, Religion, and Reality (1925), 85-148; on p. 148.

[51]This latter circumstance is evident in Roger H. Stuewer, The Compton Effect (New York: Science History Publ., 1975); the former in Jammer; and P. Forman, "The Doublet Riddle and Atomic Physics circa 1924," Isis, 1968, 59:158-174.

[52]C. G. Darwin, "The Theory of Radiation," typescript, 54 p., dated 1912 Aug. (Archive for History of Quantum Physics, microfilm 36), esp. Ch. IV, "The Conditions for a Solution," 37-46; Darwin, "A Quantum Theory of Optical Dispersion," U. S. National Acad. of Sci., Proc. 1923, 9:25-30, communicated 1922 Dec. 1, and in still briefer form in Nature, 1922, 110:841-842; "The Wave Theory and the Quantum Theory," Nature, 1923, 111:771-773.
It is true that in an unpublished paper, "The Basis of Physics," dated July 1919--quoted by Jammer, 171--Darwin had considered that, "It may be that it will prove necessary to make fundamental changes in our ideas of space and time, or to abandon the conservation of matter and electricity, or even in the last resort to endow electrons with free will." That Darwin's appeal to acausality as a last resort should be regarded as largely rhetorical, is effectively emphasized by John Hendry in his typescript "Quantum Theory and Causality before 1926." (I am grateful to Dr. Hendry for communicating his work to me prior to its publication.) So far were physicists from any serious thought of acausality at this date that even Bohr, for whose eye Darwin had drafted these notes, understood Darwin's reference to free will as simply an expression of "the often seen sentence that the electrons cannot know the final state of transition and adapt its frequency to this beforehand. . . ." (Bohr to Darwin, draft 1919 July, incomplete and unsent. Archive for History of Quantum Physics, microfilm BSC 1.)

[53]O. W. Richardson, The Electron Theory of
Matter, 2nd ed. (Cambridge, 1916), 507-508.

[54]N. Bohr, H. A. Kramers, J. C. Slater, "The
Quantum Theory of Radiation," Philos. Magazine,
1924, 47:785-802, on p. 790.

[55]Ibid.; Jammer, 171.

[56]N. R. Campbell, "Time and Chance," Philos.
Magazine, 1926, 1:1106-1117, dated 1926 Feb. 18.
Cf., Campbell, "Atomic Structure," Nature, 1920,
106:408-409; 1921, 108:170.

[57]Eddington in J. Needham, ed., Science,
Religion, and Reality (1925), 193-218. In choosing
his title Eddington was likely echoing, and thus
implicitly rebutting, Ernest Wm. Hobson's 1921/22
Gifford Lectures, The Domain of Physical Science
(Cambridge, 1923). Hobson, passing up this ideal
opportunity for repudiating causality, declared
(p. 98) that "we are not acquainted with barriers
which will prevent ever larger tracts of phenomena
from being correlated with deterministic descriptive schemes."

[58]Ibid., 211, 217-18.

[59]Ibid., 211.

[60]Eddington, "The Meaning of Matter and the
Laws of Nature according to the Theory of Relativity," Mind, 1920, 29:145-158; Space, Time, and
Gravitation (Cambridge, 1920), Preface dated May 1;
"The Philosophical Aspect of the Theory of Relativity," Mind, 1920, 29:415-422. Eight years later
Eddington recalled that "the idealistic tinge in
my conception of the physical world arose out of
mathematical researches on the relativity theory.
Insofar as I had any earlier philosophical views,
they were of an entirely different complexion."
Nature of the Physical World (Cambridge, 1928),
preface. For the several questions addressed in
this essay, Herbert Dingle's The Sources of Eddington's Philosophy (1954) is quite useless.

[61]It is likely that at this earliest stage
Weyl was already an important influence upon
Eddington. Weyl had expressed essentially this
same view of the field laws in Raum, Zeit, Materie,
which first appeared in 1918 and in its third edition late in 1919. Weyl is mentioned by Eddington
in 1920 in both physical and logical juxtaposition
to Eddington's exposition of these views.

The animus against causality seems to have
taken hold of Eddington in the summer of 1920.
In the first of his articles in Mind, published in
April, Eddington argued that the laws of mechanics,
gravity, and electricity are imposed by the mind
upon the world. He did not suggest that there is
anything oppressive in this circumstance or anything liberating to be anticipated from the discovery of "the actual order of nature," "the
genuine laws of a possibly irrational world." The
second of his articles in Mind, published in October, concluded on the contrary, that "this emanci-
pation . . . is likely to be hailed with relief."
And here again a direct influence by Weyl is certainly possible: his essay on 'the relation of the
causal to the statistical viewpoint in physics'
was published in August, 1920.

[62]Eddington, Relativity Theory of Protons
and Electrons (1936) as quoted by L. Susan Steb-
bing, Philosophy and the Physicists (London, 1937),
190.

[63]This preoccupation had not yet possessed
Eddington when, in May, 1922, he delivered the
Romanes Lecture, The Theory of Relativity and its
Influence on Scientific Thought (Oxford, 1922),
16-18. On the contrary he there placed himself
fully behind the conventional Minkowskian view that
Relativity had rendered the concept "now" com-
pletely arbitrary.

[64]J. H. Jeans, "Space, Time, and the Universe," Nature, 1926, 117:308-311. Einstein was
almost certainly not present at this 1926 Feb. 12
meeting of the RAS.

[65]L. L. Whyte, Archimedes, or The Future of
Physics (London, 1927), 9.

[66]L. L. Whyte, "Notes on scientific ideas, 1925-27" (Boston University, Mugar Library, Whyte Papers, box 38, folder 7e).

[67]Whyte, Archimedes (1927), 9, 95.

[68]Aristotelian Society, Proceedings, suppl. vol. 4 (1924), 19-49.

[69]Ibid., 22. Special mention should be made of Oliver Lodge as he held such a special place among British scientist of this period. "His bodily appearance," J. H. Muirhead opined, "is probably better known than that of any other man of our time outside the field of politics," and his outspoken belief in spiritualism made him notorious. Was he, on this latter account perhaps, an indeterminist. Far from it. Early in 1927 it was clear to him that "the present tendency admittedly is to feel . . . that the power of prediction is limited not only by our capacity, but by the nature of things, and that the uniformity of nature can be interfered with by the real agency of self-determination and free-will." (Modern Scientific Ideas, 10-11). But Lodge himself still held fast to the "faith that there is a reign of law and order." To quote once again John Henry Muirhead's Reflections by a Journeyman in Philosophy (London, 1942), 116-118, "there was more than a grain of truth in Samuel Alexander's remark to me as we once left Mariemont after a long talk with him, 'It would be an odd thing if spiritualists should turn out to be the last surviving materialists.'"

[70]M. Born, "Physical Aspects of Quantum Mechanics," Nature, 1927, 119:354-357; P. Jordan, "Philosophical Foundations of Quantum Theory," Nature, 1927, 119:566-569. Literal English translations of the titles of the original German publications in Die Naturwissenschaften would have been, respectively, "Quantum Mechanics and Statistics" and "Causality and Statistics in Modern Physics." The departures from the German titles are indicative of that very difference in focus between Germany and Britain which this essay is chiefly intended to emphasize. Born's paper was an adaptation of that which he presented at the

BA meeting in Oxford in August, 1926.  Much as we
would like to know what Born actually said on that
occasion, the pertinent fact is that whatever he
may have said seems to have remained without effect
upon his auditors.

Among the more striking of the misappre-
hended opportunities to comment in Nature upon the
epistemic issues were: the editorial attempting a
general description of the "new points . . .
raised" by Bohr's "Atomic Theory and Mechanics,"
appended to the 1925 Dec. 5 issue, points "which
seem likely to be of such general importance"
(116:809-810); the editorial on "The New Physics,"
1926 Dec. 18, rejoicing that "the transition from
the apparently unknowable to the knowable, and
from the knowable to the known, is not only rapid,
but is also undergoing a constant acceleration"
(118:865-867); H. S. Allen's notice, 1927 Jan.
15, of recent progress in quantum theory (119:77-
79).

[71]O. W. Richardson, "The Present State of
Atomic Physics," Physical Society, London, Proceedings, 1927, 39:171-186.

[72]C. G. Darwin, "The Electron as a Vector
Wave," Nature, 1927, 119:282-284.  In response
Jakov Frenkel wrote Darwin, from Leningrad, 1927
Mar. 16: "Your attempt to deal with the electron
as with a vector wave is very interesting indeed.
You will excuse me I hope for a bit of criticism:
. . . What physical meaning is to be attached to
your [vector wave] functions $f$ and $g$?" (AHQP).

[73]R. H. Fowler, "Matrix and Wave Mechanics,"
Nature, 1927, 119:239-241.

[74]N. R. Campbell, "Philosophical Foundations
of Quantum Theory," Nature, 1927, 119:779.

[75]Inferred from Campbell's correspondence
with L. L. Whyte, 1927 Nov.-Dec.  Whyte himself
had nothing against causality or determinism, and
was unimpressed by Heisenberg's uncertainty principle (Boston Univ., Mugar Library, Whyte Papers).

[76]Eddington's lectures were revised and
printed as The Nature of the Physical World

(Cambridge, 1928).

[77]Brief report of Eddington's 5th Gifford lecture, 1927 Feb. 18, in Nature, 1927, 119:328.

[78]It is consistent with the frivolity of Jeans' one anti-causal escapade, that when acausality arrived in earnest he had difficulty in accepting it: The Mysterious Universe (Cambridge, 1930), 31-32, together with Jeans' silence on the issue between 1926 and this late date.

[79]Eddington, "The Decline of Determinism," Mathematical Gazette, 1932, 16:66-80, as reprinted in Smithsonian Institution, Annual Report (1932), 141-157.

[80]Dirac's conversion occurred on the spot: Electrons et photons, 261.

[81]E.g., Henry T. Flint, Wave Mechanics (London, 1929), who was recalcitrant: Geo. P. Thomson, The Wave Mechanics of Free Electrons (New York, 1930), and H. S. Allen, Electrons and Waves (London, 1932), who were reluctantly bending.

# The Reception and Acceptance of Continental Drift Theory as a Rational Episode in the History of Science

**2**

Henry Frankel

## Introduction*

The initial rejection of continental drift theory when proposed by Wegener and Taylor in the early teens of this century, the rather hostile reception of the theory throughout the first half of the century, and its eventual acceptance in the form of seafloor spreading and plate tectonics by most geologists in the middle sixties offers historians and philosophers of science a recent and interesting case study. What is of special interest in this case study is that it is an example of an unconventional or poorly received theory which after approximately fifty years finally was accepted and embraced by the respective scientific community and is presently being used to solve numerous problems in the geological sciences. At first glance this recent revolution in the geological sciences might give those sociologists of science, who argue that acceptance and rejection of scientific theories is wholly or mostly an irrational enterprise, reason to rejoice. However, I shall explore the possibility that the history of continental drift theory can be explained as completely rational so long as close attention is paid to the historical developments involved, and narrow and mistaken analyses of rationality are eschewed. In this paper I shall

*Research on this paper was supported by funding from NEH and NSF. In addition I should like to thank Nanette Biersmith.

outline a rational account of the development and
reception of drift theory, and shall utilize the
account of scientific growth and change developed
by Larry Laudan in his Progress and Its Problems
as an heuristic aid.[1]  Overall, I shall argue that
geologists had good reason for not accepting continental drift theory until after the confirmation
of Vine-Matthews's and Wilson's transform fault
hypothesis in the middle sixties, although there
was good reason for some geologists to pursue
drift theory because they justifiably believed
that it would eventually be able to solve numerous
problems in the geological sciences--more, for that
matter, than the competing theories.  To this end
I shall briefly summarize the relevant aspects of
Laudan's account of theory choice, outline the
development of drift theory and seafloor spreading, and apply Laudan's analysis to the outlined
history of drift theory.  Finally I shall argue
that an addition must be made to Laudan's analysis
of theory choice, if it is to be fully applicable
to the reception of continental drift.

### Laudan's Analysis of Scientific
### Growth and Change

## A.   Rationality, Progress and Problem-Solving
## Effectiveness

Laudan maintains that philosophers and historians of science have failed to account for many
episodes in the history of science as rational
developments because they have either neglected
the history of science or employed too narrow a
notion of rationality.  Consequently, he develops
a broader notion of rationality and utilizes the
history of science as a test for his analysis of
scientific growth and change.  His notion of
rationality allows to taking into consideration
non-empiricist factors when choosing between or
among competing theories, and it is in this respect that his account of theory choice utilizes a
broader notion of rationality than proposed by
more empirically minded philosophers of science
such as Thomas Kuhn and Imre Lakatos, for, at
least according to Laudan, both Kuhn and Lakatos
count as rational considerations only empirical
ones.

Laudan links "making rational choices" with

"making progressive choices." He holds that a
scientist ought to choose from among a set of competing theories or research traditions that one
which is the most progressive, and that the pro-
gressiveness of a research tradition or theory is
a function of how many important empirical and
conceptual problems it is able to solve. Roughly
speaking, Laudan claims that a scientist makes a
rational choice when he decides to pursue or accept a scientific theory or research tradition
on the basis that there is good reason to suppose
that pursuit or outright acceptance of the chosen
theory or research tradition will eventually or
immediately allow him to solve more important
problems than if he had chosen to pursue or accept
one of the competing theories or traditions.

B.   Research Traditions Versus Specific Theories

Like Kuhn and Lakatos, Laudan believes that
specific scientific theories are constitutive of
broader megatheories or, in Laudan's terms, research traditions. His analysis of these megatheories differs somewhat from those put forth by
Kuhn and Lakatos. I summarize briefly his account.
First, specific scientific theories are constitutive of or make up research traditions, and specific theories should not be viewed or considered in
isolation but as part of a tradition. Second, research traditions go

> through a number of different, detailed
> (and often mutually contradictory) formu-
> lations and generally have a long history
> extending through a significant period of
> time. (By contrast, theories are fre-
> quently short-lived.)[2]

Laudan, consequently, believes that research traditions have a hard core which is that element of
the research tradition which is treated by proponents as sacrosanct. However, unlike Lakatos,
Laudan believes that the hard core of a given research tradition is not immune to change, and
often goes through alteration throughout the overall development of the tradition. What Laudan
stresses is a continuity of the hard core as
opposed to immunity from change. When uncovering
specific theories as constitutive of a given research tradition, one looks for overlaps of key
assumptions rather than identity. Third, research
traditions in and of themselves solve no empirical

or conceptual problems, although they set up a
framework wherein constitutive specific theories
are proposed as solutions to various conceptual and
empirical problems.  They provide such a framework
by delineating a set of metaphysical and methodological assumptions which are followed by proponents of the research tradition when proposing
specific theories.  Fourth, proponents of a given
research tradition attempt to improve the overall
success of their tradition by devising specific
theories in order to improve its problem-solving
effectiveness.  Here the scientist develops a new
theory so as to improve the problem-solving effectiveness of the research tradition with respect
to previous specific theories within his tradition
and with respect to contemporary specific theories
in competing research traditions.

## C.    The Objects and Modes of Theory Choice

According to Laudan, scientists choose between
and among competing research traditions and specific theories, and their basic choice is between
or among competing research traditions rather than
specific theories.  One would be much more likely
to give up a specific theory rather than a whole
tradition.

Laudan develops a distinction, implicit in
Kuhn, concerning the different ways in which a
scientist may endorse a particular research tradition; namely he may accept and pursue the tradition
or theory or he may merely pursue them without
accepting them.  Questions of theory acceptance
involve the scientist's believing that the given
research tradition or theory solves more important
problems than any of the competing specific theories constitutive of his own research tradition or
a competing one.  In contrast, when deciding to
accept a theory as the best problem-solver, a
scientist may well decide to pursue a theory or
new research tradition without accepting it.  Here
he doesn't have to believe that its problem-solving
effectiveness is better than that of the competing
theories, but only that it shows greater promise
in its future ability to solve problems than exhibited by the competing theories.

## D.  The Criterion of Theory Choice

Much has been suggested so far about Laudan's thesis that the adequacy of a tradition or specific scientific theory is a function of how many important problems it solves in comparison to the competition.  Indeed, Laudan views as central to his analysis of theory choice the thesis that scientific theories and research traditions in conjunction with specific theories are most important problem-solvers. Consequently, he develops a taxonomy of the different kinds of scientific problems, which I shall now summarize: Laudan makes an initial distinction between empirical and conceptual problems:

> Empirical problems, unlike conceptual ones, are first order problems; they are substantive questions about the objects which constitute the domain of any given science.  Unlike (conceptual problems), we judge the adequacy of solutions to empirical problems by studying the objects in the domain.[3]

Laudan suggests the following working definitions for solved, unsolved and anomalous empirical problems: solved--those which have been solved by at least one theory; unsolved--those for which there is no adequate solution; anomalous problems--those which have not been solved by at least one theory, but have been solved by at least one of the competing theories.  These working definitions highlight the fact that Laudan believes that the question of theory choice is fundamentally a comparison among competing theories, rather than a simple comparison between a theory and the data it is supposed to account for--be they facts or problems.  This is apparent from the fact that he defines the types of empirical problems in terms of whether they have been solved by at least one member of the competing set of theories or research traditions.

Of the three kinds of problems, unsolved ones are the hardest to recognize.  Laudan even suggests that:

> unsolved problem generally count as genuine problems only when they are no.

onger unsolved.  Until solved by
>me theory in a domain they are
generally only "potential" problems
rather than actual ones.[4]

Laudan holds that unsolved problems are basically
unrecognizable because there is no a priori way to
ascertain whether an unsolved problem is a genuine
problem for the theory or set of competing theories.
Often it takes "considerable time before a phenomenon is sufficiently authenticated to be taken
seriously" as a problem, and it is often "very unclear to which domain of science" a given problem
belongs.[5]  Consequently, Laudan holds that "in
appraising the relative merits of theories, the
class of unsolved problems is altogether irrelevant."[6]

Anomalous problems, however, are easily recognized since they have already been solved by at
least one but not all of a set of competing
theories or research traditions.  As Laudan emphasizes, his view of anomalies differs in two respects
from the "stabdard account."  He does not believe
that scientists should renounce a theory whenever
it is faced with an anomaly, but rather that the
"occurrence of an anomaly raises doubts about, but
need not compel the abandonment of the theory exhi-
biting the anomaly."[7]  Nor does he hold the view
that all and only empirical data which is inconsistent with a theory is anomalous, for, as follows
from his definition, any and only data which is
inexplicable for a theory but has been solved by a
competing theory is anomalous.  Laudan's first deviation from the "standard view" is quite mild--it is
questionable whether it now constitutes much of a
deviation.  His second deviation, however, is more
interesting.  What it does, besides allowing non-
inconsistent, but not all inconsistent, data to
count as anomalous, is explicitly bring into the
evaluation of theories comparison with the competition; for only data accounted for by a competing
theory can be anomalous.

A solved problem is:

In very rough form . . . an empirical
problem is solved when, within a particular context of inquiry, scientists

properly no longer regard it as an
unanswered question, i.e., when they
believe they understand why the situation propounded by the problem is the
way it is.[8]

Laudan, in explicating the notion of a 'solved
problem,' quite rightly shifts his emphasis to
'adequate solutions' since it is the solution
which makes the problem solved.

Generally, any theory, T, can be regarded as having solved an empirical
problem, if T functions (significantly)
in any schema of inference whose conclusion is a statement of the problem.[9]

Unlike traditional analyses (of 'explanation'),
Laudan's holds neither that the conclusion need be
an exact statement of the problem nor that the
premises must be true.  He argues that solutions
can range with respect to their accuracy, and
that the truth of a theory is irrelevant to the
effectiveness of the theory as a solution.  Where
Laudan lays stress on the adequacy of a specific
solution to solve a problem is in its ability to
solve the problem(s) for which it is designed
without generating conceptual and anomalous empirical problems.  At bottom, the reason why Laudan
considers truth to be irrelevant and exactness not
necessary for the adequacy of a theory is that he
wants his criterion of theory choice to be one
which can (and has been) used in the making of
theory choices.  Since exactness is rare and truth
unattainable, he basically eliminates them as
necessary conditions for an adequate solution.
This desiredutility of a criterion for theory
choice is also part of the reason why Laudan places
so much importance on the overall problem-solving
effectiveness of individual theories.  He believes
that the additional problems generated by a solution can be counted and ranked in importance.

Of the three empirical problems, unsolved
ones count little in theory evaluation.  Anomalous
and solved empirical ones are much more important.
The comparative value of the different kinds of
empirical problems can be easily understood from
the following:[10]

1.  Suppose problem p is unsolved with
    respect to a set of competing theories.
    Since unsolved problems are really only
    problems when solved it is of little
    detriment to any of the theories that
    it has not solved p.

2.  Suppose p is solved by one of the com-
    peting theories. p is then a solved
    problem with respect to the solving
    theory, and p is an anomalous problem
    with respect to the remaining theories.
    It is an epistemic plus for the solving
    theory and a detriment for those theories
    offering no solution.

3.  Suppose p, <u>qua</u> anomalous problem, is
    solved by another theory. Such an
    accomplishment is a double bonus for
    the theory since it is more to the
    credit of a theory to solve an anomaly
    than an unsolved problem. When an
    anomaly is solved a deficiency is
    turned into a plus; when an unsolved
    problem is solved only a plus is added
    since there is no detriment to remove.

The locus of Laudan's expanded notion of
rationality as relevant to theory choice is in his
inclusion of conceptual problems as a relevant
concern for theory choice. According to Laudan
an unfelicitous result of this general underesti-
mation of the importance of conceptual problems
is that methodologists--Laudan here includes Feyer-
abend, Kuhn and Lakatos in this group--"find themselves too impoverished to explain or reconstruct
much of the actual history of science," and have
no way of explaining why one theory or tradition
replaces another in cases where the theories have
approximately the same effectiveness in solving
empirical problems.[11] Consequently, given their
methodologies, many episodes in the history of
science seem imbued with irrationality.

Laudan distinguishes between external and
internal conceptual problems. Internal conceptual
problems arise for a theory or research tradition
when it "exhibits certain internal inconsistencies,
or when its basic categories of analysis are vague
and unclear"; external conceptual problems result

from conflicts between the given theory or research
tradition and some other theory or doctrine which
is taken to be rationally well founded.[12]  These
external conceptual problems in general arise
when the actual relations which obtain between
theories are not as intimate as expected, and
Laudan distinguishes three general cases: (1)
When the new theory is logically inconsistent with
an established one, e.g., Copernican astronomy
with Ptolemaic astronomy.  (2) Where, although
there is no inconsistency, the two theories seem
implausible.  Here the established theory doesn't
make it impossible or deny that the new theory
can hold; but it does make it implausible, e.g.,
late seventeenth century theories of physiology
based upon Cartesian mechanism and Newtonian
physics.  (3) "When a theory emerges which ought to
reinforce another theory, but fails to do so and
is merely compatible with it."[13]  This is perhaps
the most interesting case discussed by Laudan.  In
this situation, support is expected from an established theory, but the support is not forthcoming.

### Historical Analysis of the Development of Drift Theory

A.  ### The Early and Middle Career of Drift

Although two Americans, Baker and Taylor,
developed versions of drift, Alfred Wegener was
the first to propose an extensive version of drift
tradition.  (Hereafater, I shall refer to the drift
tradition as DRIFT).  He did so in 1915 with the
publication of his book Die Entstehung der Kontinente und Ozeane.[14]

The basic tenets of Wegener's theory are
easily summarized.  Wegener regarded the continents
as ships of light sialic material floating upon a
heavier basaltic material which formed the ocean
floor.  He proposed that the continents underwent
horizontal displacement by ploughing through the
denser baslatic ocean floor.  During the carboni-
ferous period, all the continents were united together forming a supercontinent which Wegener
called 'Pangea.'  Pangea began to break up during
late cretaceous or early tertiary times.  By
eocene times North and South America had broken
away from Europe and Africa, opening up the

Atlantic Ocean, and Asia had moved away from Antarctica and southern Africa by migrating northward
and rotating counterclockwise.  By the beginning
of quarternary times Australia finally split off
from Antarctica, the Americas continued to migrate
westward, and Asia continued to drift and rotate.

Wegener argued that his version of DRIFT
offered solutions to the following empirical problems:

1.    Why the contours of the coastlines of eastern
South America and western Africa fit together so
well, and why there were many similarities between
the respective coastlines of North America and
Europe.  Here his solution was simply to postulate
that the continents had originally been one land-
mass.

2.    Why there were numerous geological similarities between Africa and South America, and others
between North America and Europe.  Wegener here
appealed to similarities in the Cape mountains of
South Africa and the sierras of Buenos Aires,
numerous similarities in the huge gneiss plateaux
of Brazil and Africa and the pleistocene terminal
moraines.  He also spoke of the continuity of the
three major systems of folds between North America
and Europe, viz., the Armorican, Caledonian and
Algonkian, so as to extend his thesis to North
America and Europe.  Finally, Wegener cited similarities in the geological structure of India,
Antarctica, Australia, New Zealand and New Guinea,
in an attempt to show that his version of DRIFT
accounted for many geological problems.  Again
Wegener simply argued that the previous joining of
the continents solved the problems.

3.    Why the paleontological record indicated that
many plant and animal species had lived in both
South America and Africa prior to the paleozoic
and why the record also indicated that the presence
of similar species decreased enormously after the
paleozoic.  Here Wegner argued that the problem
could be solved by supposing that the continents
had been joined prior to the paleozoic and then
had subsequently separated.  Wegener also argued
that the evidence in favor of his drift theory was
enhanced by the fact that it solved problems (1)
through (3) with respect to South America and

Africa.

> Even though the theory (Wegener's
> theory) in certain individual cases may
> still be uncertain, the totality of
> these points of correspondence consti-
> tutes an almost incontrovertible proof
> of the correctness of our belief that
> the Atlantic is to be regarded as an
> expanded rift.  Of crucial importance
> here is the fact that, although the blocks
> must be rejoined on the basis of other
> features--their outlines, especially--the
> conjunction brings the continuation of
> each formation on the farther side into
> perfect contact with the end of the forma-
> tion on the near side.  It is just as if
> we were to refit the torn pieces of a
> newspaper by matching their edges and then
> check whether the lines of print run
> smoothly across.  If they do, there is
> nothing left but to conclude that the
> pieces were in fact joined in this way.
> If only one line was available for the
> test, we would still have found a high
> probability for the accuracy of fit, but
> if we have n lines, this probability is
> raised to the nth power.  It is certainly
> of some value to make the significance of
> this clear.  Let us assume that we can
> bet ten to one on the correctness of drift
> theory just on the first 'line' alone--
> the folding of the Cape mountains and the
> Sierras of Buenos Aires; then, since there
> are at least six such independent tests
> available, we can bet a million ($10^6$) to
> one on the theory being right, in view of
> our knowledge of the six tests.  These
> figures may be regarded as exaggerated,
> but they should show the significance of
> a plurality of independent tests.[15]

4.   Why mountain ranges were usually located along
the coast lines of continents, and why orogenic
regions were long and narrow in shape.

> . . . continental drift is linked casu-
> ally with orogenesis.  In the westward
> drift of both Americas their leading
> edges were compressed and folded by the

frontal resistance of the ancient
Pacific floor, which was deeply chilled
and hence a source of viscous drag.  The
result was the vast Andean range which ex-
tends from Alaska to Antarctica.  Consider
also the case of the Australian block, including New Guinea, which is separated only
by shelf sea: on the leading side, relative
to the direction of displacement one finds
the high-altitude New Guinea range, a recent
formation. . . .The present-day coast line
was then the leading side. . . .The present-
day cordilleran system of eastern Australia
was formed in still earlier times; it arose
at the same time as the earlier folds in
South and North America, which formed the
basis of the Andes (pre-cordilleras), at
the leading edge of the continental blocks
then drifting as a whole before dividing.[16]

While the Himalayas, he argued, which are not along
a coastline, had formed when India had slid into
and under Asia.

5.    Why the earth's crust exhibited two basic
elevations, one corresponding to the elevation of
the continental tables, the other to the ocean
floors.  Here Wegener argued that "there simply
were at one time two undisturbed primal levels"
which have remained relatively unchanged, since,
according to his theory the major diastrophic
disturbances were horizontal rather than vertical.

6.    How to account for the Permo-Carboniferous
moraine deposits found in South Africa, Argentina,
southern Brazil, India and in western, central,
and eastern Australia.  Wegener's solution was
simply to suppose that the respective continents
had been united during the Permo-Carboniferous
period and that there had been an extensive ice-
cap during the Permo-Carboniferous period.

Wegener, besides pointing out how his theory
solved these above-mentioned empirical problems,
argued that his theory offered better solutions
to many of the above problems than competing
theories.  Briefly, the main thrust of Wegener's
argument centered around his claim that competing
theories either had solutions saddled with conceptual problems or no solution at all.  For

example, he argued that those theorists who believed that the continents had not moved horizontally and who hypothesized the existence of former
landbridges to account for the respective paleontological similarities had foisted upon themselves a
conceptual problem, namely, that there was no known
mechanism for the sinking of the supposed landbridges back into the ocean floor once they had
served as migratory routes which was consistent
with the principle of isostasy.  Those theorists
who rejected the previous existence of landbridges
as a solution to the paleontological problems
because of its inconsistency with the principle of
isostasy, and believed in the permanency of the
continents and oceans had no solution whatsoever.

> However, where does the truth lie?  The
> earth at any one time can only have had
> one configuration.  Were there land bridges
> then, or were the continents separated by
> broad stretches of ocean, as today?  It is
> impossible to deny the postulate of former
> land bridges if we do not want to abandon
> wholly the attempt to understand the evolu-
> tion of life on earth.  But it is also
> impossible to overlook the grounds on which
> the exponents of permanence deny the exis-
> tence of sunken intermediate continents
> (if we do not want to abandon the generally
> held principle of isostasy).  There clearly
> remains but one possibility: there must be
> a hidden error in the assumptions alleged
> to be obvious.[17]

Besides pointing out the benefits of his theory
Wegener admitted that it was faced with its own
conceptual problem for which he offered tentative
solutions and attempted to play down its importance.  The problem in Wegener's terms was that
there was no known force sufficient to propel the
continents such vast distances through the ocean
floor.  Given the views concerning the ridigity
of the earth, Wegener had to propose some mechanism for the drifting of the continents, or at
least show it was possible for the continents to
move through the seafloor.  He suggested two
mechanisms which might be responsible for the
horizontal displacement, namely tidal and pole-
flight force.  Pohlflucht is a differential gravitational force due to the elliptical shape of the

earth. The continents would tend to move toward the equator through the action of centrifugal force brought about by the spinning and shape of the earth. The centrifugal force would cause the continents to move away from the center of the earth. Thus, the continents supposedly would flee from the poles, since the equatorial radius of the earth is larger than the polar radius. Tidal force, on the other hand, was taken by Wegener to provide the requisite westward drift of the continents. These tidal forces were actually stresses brought about by the gravitational action of the sun and the moon. Wegener claimed that these tidal stresses, which slowed the earth's diurnal eastward motion, would act most strongly on the surface of the earth. As a result, their action would lead to "a slow sliding motion of the whole crust or of the individual continental blocks" in a westward direction.[18]   In addition, Wegener, in his 1929 edition of The Origin of Continents and Oceans, attempted to ameliorate the seriousness of the mechanism objection.

> The Newton of drift theory has not yet appeared. His absence need cause no anxiety; the theory is still young and still often treated with suspicion. In the long run, one cannot blame a theoretician for hesitating to spend time and trouble on explaining a law about whose validity no unanimity prevails. It is probable, at any rate, that the complete solution of the problem of the driving forces will still be a long time coming, for it means the unravelling of a whole tangle of interdependent phenomena, where it is often hard to distinguish what is cause and what is effect.[19]

The reception to Wegener's version of DRIFT was extremely unfavorable. Only a few geologists endorsed the theory. In general the substantive aspects of the criticisms were of three varieties. First, critics argued that some of the empirical problems for which Wegener had found solutions were merely pseudo-problems. Second, opponents argued that their own theories provided equally as good or better solutions to some of the empirical

problems.  Third, and most important, critics
argued that the conceptual problem of finding a
mechanism for DRIFT compatible with the estimated
rigidity of the earth was insurmountable.  In short,
critics argued that Wegener had grossly overesti-
mated the problem-solving effectiveness of his
version of DRIFT; that it created more difficulties
than it solved.

The most serious of these attacks was the
conceptual one concerning the proposed mechanism
for DRIFT.  There were, I believe, three reasons
for why this criticism carried such weight.  First,
the mechanism problem was directed at the hard
core of Wegener's theory, namely that the continents had displaced themselves horizontally by
ploughing through the seafloor.  This idea was at
the heart of Wegener's theory; it served as a
crucial premise in every one of his empirical solutions except the one concerning the two basic elevations of the earth's crust.  Second, no tradition
except DRIFT proposed lengthy horizontal movement
of the continents because of its conceptual difficulties.  Third, this mechanism objection was actually more extensive than originally suggested by
Wegener.  Wegener originally viewed the problem as
simply finding forces sufficiently strong enough to
propel the continents, but critics were quick to
point out that the problem also concerned, among
other things, whether the continents could survive
such vast movements without crumbling, regardless
of whether there were sufficient forces to propel
them.

So as to get an appreciation for the seriousness of this 'mechanism' objection, consider the
following brief account of its development: P. Lake
initiated the attack in his 1911 review of the 2nd
edition of Wegener's work by questioning the ade-
qucy of Wegener's proposed forces.

> But Wegener imagines that these lighter
> masses [the continents] have moved later-
> ally, and are still moving, and this is a
> very different matter.  There is the force
> of gravity to press them downwards into the
> Sima, but there is no known force comparable
> in magnitude with this to move them sideways.[20]

Admittedly, Lake softened his complaint by admit-
ting the possibility of some unknown force.

It is possible, however, that a much
smaller force may be sufficient, for
the movements imagined are imperceptibly
slow and the time allowed indefinitely
long.[21]

Indeed, Wegener had suggested that if the
forces were too weak to move the continents in a
short amount of time, that given enough time even
small forces could displace the continents. However, Harold Jeffreys, who became one of the most
influential of geophysicists with the publication
of The Earth in 1924 allowed Wegener no such exit.

A further impossible hypothesis has often
been associated with hypotheses of continental drift and with other geological
hypotheses based on the conception of the
earth as devoid of strength. That is,
that the small force can not only produce
indefinitely great movement, given a long
enough time, but that it can overcome a
force many times greater acting in the
opposite direction for the same time. In
Wegener's theory, for instance . . . the
assumption that the earth can be deformed
indefinitely by small forces, provided
only that they act long enough is therefore,
a very dangerous one, and liable to lead to
serious error.[22]

Jeffreys was also greatly instrumental in
developing another addition to the 'mechanism'
objection--namely, that the continents would dis-
integrate rather than remain intact, since seafloor material is stronger than continental
material. Jeffreys first offered this objection
in 1922 at the meeting of the Geological Section
of the British Association. W. B. Wright summarized Jeffreys' objections in his report in Nature.

Dr. Harold Jeffreys stated that the rota-
tional force which could be invoked to
explain the movements of the continents
were very small and quite insufficient to
produce the crumpling up of the Pacific
ranges. The ocean floors also presented a
difficulty, for being composed of basaltic
rock, they would be less radioactive and

therefore stronger than the continental crust.[23] (My italics)

As far as Jeffreys was concerned, having the continents plough their way through the seafloor would
be like attempting to thrust a leaden chisel into
steel.

Wegener and some of his followers offered a
reply to this objection, but their answer carried
little weight.  Basically, they argued for a distinction between residual rigidity or strength
and rigidity or plasticity.  At the AAPG (American
Association of Petroleum Geologists) Symposium Van
der Gracht argued as follows:[24]

> This . . . [objection depends upon]
> . . . the usual misconception concerning
> the physical properties of matter which
> apply to this problem: a confusion of
> "rigidity" with "residual rigidity" or
> "strength."  The sima has greater "rigidity"
> than the sial, but the latter, as a whole,
> evidently has greater "strength."  That
> is, it has a greater resistance against
> long enduring stresses. . . . Whether a
> substance is "hard" or "soft," like steel
> or lead, has not necessarily anything to
> do with its "strength."  In looking at
> similes, substances should be used whose
> properties are more within our grasp, be-
> cause we can handle them under room tem-
> perature, and ordinary pressures and time
> intervals.  So I shall refer again to bees-
> wax and pitch. Pitch has great "rigidity"
> . . . but extremely little "strength."
> While beeswax has little rigidity, but
> considerable strength.  We can perfectly
> well press a chisel of soft beeswax into
> a block of hard pitch, provided we push
> in our chisel slowly enough. That is what
> happens both in an isostatic adjustment
> and at the front of a continent floating
> forward into the sima.[25]

Although this ploy allowed for the possibility of
drift, it gained little support among opponents.
First, as Wegener admitted, there was not any hard
viscosity data.

We should not be dogmatic about the
viscosity coefficient of the earth's
interior and in particular that of the
individual layers, because we still know
nothing about it.[26]

Second, by the time of the 1926 AAPG Symposium
others had expanded the 'mechanism' objection.  At
the symposium Baily Willis and William Bowie
argued that seismological studies indicated a sima
with great residual rigidity let alone more rigidity; that tidal forces would act more strongly on
the sima rather than the sial since the former was
denser than the latter; and that if the continents
were to drift, their trailing edges would split
apart through the action of strong tensional forces.

Other versions of DRIFT made their appearance
in the twenties and thirties.  John Joly proposed
a sketch as early as 1923.  Joly argued that pole-
flight and tidal forces were, ceteris paribus, too
weak to displace the continents through the ocean
floor.  But, he suggested that the seafloor might
on occasion weaken from the release of heat caused
by radioactivity at which time the combined action
of tidal and precessional forces might propel the
continents.[27]  In 1937, Alex du Toit, a South
African geologist, presented an alternative history
for the breakup of the continents, and attempted
to correct many of Wegener's mistakes in outlining
the geological similarities between Africa and
South America,[28] while in 1928 and later in 1931
Arthur Holmes presented a detailed alternative
version of DRIFT which was designed to circumvent
the mechanism problems.[29]  During the late teens
and early twenties Holmes had become disenchanted
with the contractionist model for the earth's
history primarily because the abundance of radioactivity in the earth's crust and upper mantle
provided too much heat for the earth to contract
from cooling.  Holmes, then, impressed with the
ability of DRIFT to solve the above mentioned
empirical problems--especially the one concerned
with the Permo-Carboniferous Icecap--developed an
alternative version of DRIFT.  In his view the
continents were displaced by convection currents
fueled by heat generated through radioactivity.
Moreover, Holmes' version of DRIFT did not require
that the continents ploughed their way through the
seafloor.  Rather, his proposal, which we may call

'seafloor thinning,' had the continents separate
from one another as a rising limb of a convection
cell turned along the horizontal and stretched
out the simatic layer of the crust and upper mantle,
i.e., the seafloor.  Consequently, the continents
did not plough their way through the seafloor but
were carried along with it.  Although Holmes'
version of DRIFT brought about an admission on the
part of Jeffreys that DRIFT was no longer an impossibility, Jeffreys argued that the chances of
the appropriate convection currents arising was
extremely unlikely.  In 1931, at a discussion of
the Geography Section of the British Association,
which was entitled "Problems of the Earth's Crust,"
Jeffreys said in the presence of Holmes:

> I have examined Professor Holmes' theory
> of subcrustal currents to some extent, and
> have not found any test that appears de-
> cisive for or against.  So far as I can
> see there is nothing inherently impossible
> in it, but the association of the condi-
> tions that would be required to make it
> work would be rather in the nature of a
> fluke. . . . For the theory [Holmes'
> hypothesis] to succeed would require the
> currents to be in the same direction over
> regions of continental dimensions; that is,
> the instability developed must correspond
> to the lowest mode of disturbance and no
> other.  If the supply of heat was greater
> than could be carried off by the motions
> of small extend, resembling those that
> occur in the boiling of a kettle, and
> these would be no use for producing wide-
> spread geological effects.

## B.   The Later Career of DRIFT

During the forties DRIFT gained few advocates.
Wegener died in 1930, and Holmes, Du Toit and
others continued to support the tradition.  But in
1944 Baily Willis argued that DRIFT should be
leveled the deathblow since it was an obstruction
to knowledge, and the apparent confirmation of the
westward drift of Greenland by the Danish Geodetic
Institute was shown to be incorrect by Longwell.[31]
In short, proponents of DRIFT weren't greatly im-
proving its problem-solving ability, and DRIFT, if
anything, lost ground as an acceptable theory among

members of the geological community.

DRIFT, however, had a resurgence in the late fifties through its ability to offer solutions to empirical problems arising through paleomagnetic studies, and in the late sixties it became the established tradition within the geological community, through the confirmation of Harry Hess' version of DRIFT, labeled by Dietz as 'seafloor spreading.'[32] Hess' version of DRIFT was able to offer solutions to numerous problems which arose through empirical studies in oceanography and paleomagnetism.

In 1960 Hess proposed that the seafloor was created at midocean ridges, spread out toward the trenches, and then descended into the mantle. He then related his model for seafloor spreading to DRIFT by suggesting that the continents were carried along by the spreading seafloor.

> . . . a continent's leading edges are strongly deformed when they impinge upon the downward moving limbs of convecting mantle . . . [that] Rising limbs coming up under continental areas move the fragmented parts away from one another at a uniform rate so a truly median ridge forms as in the Atlantic Ocean . . . [and that] The cover of oceanic sediments and the volcanic seamounts also ride down into the jaw crusher of the descending limb, are metamorphosed, and eventually probably are welded onto continents.[33]

And

> Paleomagnetic data presented by Runcorn (1959), Irving (1959) and others strongly suggest that the continents have moved by large amounts in geologically comparatively recent times. One may quibble over the details but the general picture on paleomagneticism is sufficiently compelling that it is much more reasonable to accept it than to disregard it. . . . This strongly indicates independent movement in direction and amount of large portions of the Earth's surface with respect to the rotational axis. This could be most easily accomplished

by a convecting mantle system which
involves actual movement of the Earth's
surface passively riding on the upper
part of the convecting cell.[34]

In addition, Hess claimed that his version of DRIFT
avoided the recalcitrant 'mechanism' problems.

The mid-ocean ridges could represent the
traces of the rising limbs of convection
cells while the circum-Pacific belt of
deformation and volcanism represents
descending limbs. The Mid-Atlantic Ridge
is median because the continental areas on
each side of it have moved away from it
at the same rate. . . . This is not exactly
the same as continental drift. The continents do not plow through oceanic crust
impelled by unknown forces, rather they
ride passively on mantle material as it
comes to the surface at the crest of the
ridge and then moves laterally away from
it.[35]

It is beyond question that Hess' proposal related
together a vast variety of data, and thereby
turned much puzzling data into solved problems.
His model of seafloor spreading made sense out of
such items as the following: the median position
of the ridges, the occurrence of shallow earthquakes along the ridges, the high temperature of
the ridges, and their apparent ephemeral nature,
the negative gravity anomalies along the trenches,
their cold temperature, and the occurrence of
intermediate and deep earthquakes at trench sites,
apparent transcurrent faulting off the California
coast, the uniform thickness of the bottom crustal
layer, and the widening of the fracture zone along
the Mid-Atlantic Ridge as it crosses Iceland.
Without providing support, I think it is beyond
question that Hess' version of DRIFT, or others
rather similar to it, were the only theories which
could turn this data into a nest of solved problems, and consequently these solved problems were
anomalous for the competing theories. But never-
theless, the geological community did not embrace
DRIFT after his theory became well-known through
Dietz's 1961 version which appeared in _Nature_.
Even many personnel at Lamont (Lamont-Doherty Institute since 1969) who had supplied Hess with the

oceanographic data through the work of Maurice
Ewing and others were adamantly opposed to DRIFT.

Those in the geological community who were
working in oceanography accepted DRIFT only after
the confirmation of the work by Vine, Matthews, and
Wilson.  In September of 1963 Vine and Matthews
suggested that, <u>ceteris paribus</u>, if seafloor spreading were occurring then there should be strips of
seafloor material having reverse polarity spreading out symmetrically and parallel to the ridges.
Moreover, they argued that their hypothesis

> is consistent with, in fact virtually a
> corollary of, current ideas on ocean
> floor spreading and periodic reversals in
> the Earth's magnetic field.  If the main
> crustal layer (Seismic layer 3) of the
> oceanic crust is formed over a convective
> up-current in the mantle at the centre of
> an oceanic ridge, it will be magnetized
> in the current direction of the Earth's
> field.  Assuming impermanence of the
> ocean floor, the whole of the oceanic
> crust is comparatively young, probably not
> older than 150 million years, and the
> thermo-remanent component of its magneti-
> zation is therefore either essentially
> normal, or reversed with respect to the
> present field of the Earth.  Thus, if
> spreading of the ocean floor occurs, blocks
> of alternately normal and reversely magne-
> tized material would drift away from the
> centre of the ridge and parallel to the
> crest of it.[36]

When Vine and Matthews introduced their hypothesis,
there was not enough analyzed data available to
test it.  The first profiles by Lamont personnel
were taken off the Mid-Atlantic Ridge, and the
interpretation of the profiles was taken to be
inconsistent with Vine-Matthews.  Heirtzler and Le
Pichon reported their findings in the following:

> Vine and Matthews (1963) have hypothe-
> sized that the whole ocean crust is made
> of striped material parallel to the ridge
> axis, having alternately reversed and
> normal magnetization.  They see their
> hypothesis as a corollary of the 'spreading

floor' hypothesis of Dietz (1961). . . .
If is clear from this study that most of
the profiles do not follow the pattern
assumed by Vine and Matthews.[37]

But, by the end of 1966, analyses of several profiles from the Pacific-Antarctic Ridge--especially,
Eltamin-19--and the Reykjanes Ridge supplied the
confirmatory data.[38]  Walter Pitman, the person
primarily responsible for the cleanest profile,
Eltamin-19, has said the following in retrospect:

> It hit me like a hammer. . . . In retro-
> spect, we were lucky to strike a place
> where there are no hindrances to sea-floor
> spreading.  We don't get profiles quite
> that perfect from any other place.  There
> were no irregularities to distract or de-
> ceive us.  That was good, because by then
> people had been shot down an awful lot
> over sea-floor spreading.  I had thought
> Vine and Matthews was a fairly dubious hypo-
> thesis at the time, and Fred Vine has told
> me he was not wholly convinced of his own
> theory until he saw Eltanin-19.  It does
> grab you.  It looks very much like the way
> a profile ought to look and never does.
> On the other hand, when another man here
> saw it his remark was "Next thing, you'll
> be proving Vine and Matthews."  Actually,
> it was this remark that made me go back
> and read Vine and Matthews.  We began to
> examine Eltamin-19, and we realized that
> it looked very much like a profile that
> Vine and Tuzo Wilson published just before
> our data came out of the computer.[39]

This particular profile, Eltamin-19, convinced most
personnel at Lamont that Hess' version of DRIFT
was worthy of concentrated pursuit, if not outright
acceptance.  The data from the Atlantic which had
been taken to be inconsistent with Vine-Matthews
was reinterpreted in light of Eltamin-19, and it
was now seen to be consistent with the general idea
of seafloor spreading.  In addition, seismologists
at Lamont, excited about Eltamin-19, turned to
their data to determine if they could find support
for T. Wilson's work on transform faults, which
like Vine and Matthews was a virtual corollary of
Hess' DRIFT.

In 1965 Tuzo Wilson, beginning with the
notion of seafloor spreading, reasoned that the
faulting which would occur if seafloor spreading
takes place should be transform rather than transcurrent.  He described transform faults in the
following terms:

> Faults in which the displacement suddenly
> stops or changes form and direction are
> not true transcurrent faults.  It is pro-
> posed that a separate class of horizontal
> shear faults exists which terminate abruptly
> at both ends, but which nevertheless may
> show great displacements. . . . The name
> transform fault is proposed for the class.
> . . . The distinctions between (transform
> and transcurrent faults) might appear
> trivial until the variation in habit of
> growth of the different types if considered.
> . . . These distinctions are that ridges
> expand to produce new crust, thus leaving
> residual inactive traces in the topography
> of their former positions.  On the other
> hand oceanic crust moves down under island
> arcs absorbing old crust so that they leave
> no traces of past positions.[40]

Moreover, he explicitly linked his hypothesis with
DRIFT.

> Transform faults cannot exist unless there
> is crustal displacement and their exist-
> ence would provide a powerful argument in
> favor of continental drift and a guide to
> the nature of the displacement involved.[41]

Once Vine-Matthews was confirmed, seismologists at
Lamont, who had seen the confirmatory profiles and
were quite impressed with their quality, set out
to test Wilson's hypothesis.  They obtained their
confirmatory results in 1967.  I cite the following
passage from a joint paper by the seismologists at
Lamont who confirmed Wilson's hypothesis in order
to summarize the role and confirmation of Hess'
version of DRIFT:

> The remarkable success with which the
> hypothesis of sea-floor spreading accom-
> modated such diverse geologic observa-
> tions as the linear magnetic anomalies

of the ocean (Vine and Matthews 1963)
and (Pitman and Heirtzler 1966), the
topography of the ocean floor (Menard 1965),
the distribution and configuration of
continental margins and various other land
patterns (Wilson, 1965a; Bullard et al.
1965) and certain aspects of deep-sea
sediments (Ewing and Ewing, 1967) raised
the hypothesis to a level of great importance and still greater promise.  The contributions of seismology to this development have been substantial, not only in
the form of general information on earth
structure but also in the form of certain
studies that bear especially on this hypothesis.  Two specific examples are Sykes'
(1967) evidence on seismicity patterns and
focal mechanisms to support the transform
fault hypothesis of Wilson (1965a) and
Oliver and Isack's (1967) discovery of
anomalous zones that appear to correspond
to underthrust lithosphere in the mantle
beneath island arcs.[42]

## Application of Laudan's Analysis of Scientific Growth and Change to the Development of DRIFT[43]

If Laudan's analysis is applicable to the
development and reception of DRIFT, the following
theses should hold:

Thesis 1:  There should be a continental drift research tradition wherein proponents of specific
drift theories attempt to improve the overall
problem-solving effectiveness of the tradition by
proposing specific theories.  They should argue
that their tradition solves empirical problems
without generating conceptual ones, and that it
solves more important empirical ones without creating as many conceptual problems as the competition.

Thesis 2:  DRIFT should not be accepted by the
relevant scientific community if it does not have
greater problem-solving effectiveness than competing traditions, and should be pursued only by
those scientists who believe it has promise of its
future ability to solve problems.

Thesis 3:   Once DRIFT has demonstrated its superior
ability to solve empirical problems without pro-
ducing significant conceptual ones, it should be
accepted and pursued by the community of earth
scientists.

I shall argue that Laudan's analysis as presently constituted, given this limited account,
finds support for theses 1 and 2 but fails with 3.

If this partial case study supports thesis 1,
there should be a drift tradition.  Its proponents
should argue in favor of the tradition by demonstrating its problem solving effectiveness and
propose new special theories of DRIFT to improve
its problem-solving ability.  A DRIFT tradition has
been identified and at least some of its proponents
clearly argued for DRIFT in terms of its effectiveness to solve empirical problems without generating serious conceptual ones.  Wegener identified the empirical problems for which his version
of DRIFT offered solutions, and attempted to mini-
mize the significance of the 'mechanism' problem.
Likewise Van der Gracht, although he offered no
original version of DRIFT spent considerable time
attempting to buttress Wegener's solutions to a
number of empirical problems, and highlighted a
distinction between residual rigidity and (instan-
taneous) rigidity in order to aid DRIFT in handling
the mechanism problem.  Holmes, impressed with the
promise of DRIFT to solve a nest of empirical problems, and dissatisfied with the contracting model
of the earth, turned his attention to DRIFT.  In
the spirit of pursuit, he developed a solution to
the mechanism problem, which, although it failed
to secure many new advocates to DRIFT, lessened
the mechanism objection to one of implausibility
from one of impossibility.  Du Toit, who had first-
hand knowledge of the geographies of western Africa
and eastern South America, though Wegener's theory
worthy of pursuit and even acceptance, and consequently attempted to shore up many of Wegener's
empirical solutions concerned with the geography,
geology, paleontology and paleoclimatology of the
southern hemisphere.  He also welcomed improvements
in the mechanism problem, incorporating them into
his own version of DRIFT.  Even Harry Hess, who
like Holmes was not originally a proponent of DRIFT
argued that his model for seafloor spreading had
as a direct consequence the drifting of the

continents in directions similar to those proposed
by DRIFTers, that his model offered an answer to
the mechanism problem, and that the data on continental remanent paleomagnetism--although ambigu-
ous--was supportive of DRIFT.

Moreover, even this partial case study allows
for identification of a hard core to DRIFT and
offers the opportunity to examine a changing hard
core.  The hard core of Wegener's version of DRIFT
was as follows:

1.  The continents originally formed a single
    continent, broke up during the end of the
    Cretaceous, and migrated to heir present
    positions.
2.  The continents made of material lighter
    than the ocean floor ploughed their way
    through the ocean floor as they drifted
    to their present positions.

And, by 1929 Wegner, although he didn't deny (2),
was not very sanguine about it--"The Newton of
drift theory has not yet appeared."  Thus, Wegener,
for all practical purposes, had given up (2) as
constitutive of his hard core by 1929.  The hard
core of Du Toit's theory may be expressed as follows:

The continents originally formed two super-
continents, which both began to break apart
during the Cretaceous.  The separate landmasses continued to migrate to their present
positions.

Du Toit believed that some other mechanism than the
one proposed by Wegener was needed, and was sympathetic to the mechanism put forth by Holmes.  However, he wasn't particularly settled on a definite
mechanism.  Holmes' version of DRIFT had as a hard
core:

1.  The continents originally formed two
    super-continents, which both began to
    break apart during the Cretaceous.  The
    separate landmasses continued to migrate
    to their present positions.
2.  The continents move passively on top of
    the upper mantle and lower layer of crust
    as seafloor is stretched due to convection
    currents.

Holmes, at least in the later presentations of his version of DRIFT preferred Du Toit's drifting pattern to that of Wegener's, and replaced Wegener's mechanism with his own.  The hard core of Hess' version of DRIFT was:

1.  New seafloor is created at the ridges, spreads symmetrically outward from the ridges and eventually sinks back into the mantle forming trenches.
2.  The drifting of the continents in a pattern similar to those proposed by DRIFTers is a consequence of seafloor spreading.

Indeed, there is appreciable overlap, and the replacements were offered in part as improvement over what they replaced.  In addition, the replacements accent the concern and expertise of the particular scientist.  Du Toit's primary considerations were directed toward providing a better fit of the continents than Wegener had proposed. Holmes was a geophysicist, and although impressed with the promise of DRIFT, agreed with those critics who argued that Wegener's mechanism was untenable.  Thus he developed a new mechanism. Hess was an oceanographer who was concerned with developing a model for the history of the ocean basins.  But, he realized that his model had as a direct consequence continental drift, and that it alleviated the seriousness of the conceptual problem which had plagued DRIFTers from the beginning.

Thesis 2 is the negative aspect of Laudan's analysis of theory choice.  A scientific community should not accept a tradition if its problem-solving ability is not as good as any of its competitors.  This particular case study is not extensive enough to test thesis 2 fully, but, I think it is complete enough to offer initial support. Opponents to DRIFT, certainly up to the time of Hess' version, argued that the problem-solving effectiveness of DRIFT was not nearly as strong as argued by Wegener, Du Toit and even Holmes.  Since the mechanism objections were directed to the heart of Wegener's DRIFT, they argued that DRIFT solutions to the numerous empirical problems were of little value.[44]  Furthermore, opponents claimed that their own traditions--which I have not delineated--had solutions to many of the problems

discussed by Wegener and other DRIFTers, and that
their own solutions did not bring about conceptual
problems as serious as those mechanistic ones
directed against DRIFT.  Wegener viewed his theory
as solving problems and creating anomalies for the
competitors; the competitors saw Wegener and other
DRIFTers as either solving pseudo-problems or unable to solve problems, while, they, on the other
hand, were able to solve problems.  For example,
proponents of the landbridge hypothesis offered
mechanisms for their sinking which were not incompatible with the principle of isostasy, and those
who did not believe in the existence of landbridges attempted to solve the paleontological
problems by using isthmian connections as migratory pathways.

After Holmes' work became well-known through
its inclusion in his popular textbook on physical
geology, the geological community was still un-
receptive to DRIFT.  But, again, as illustrated by
Jeffreys' remarks on Holmes' version of DRIFT:
Given Holmes, DRIFT was no longer impossible, although it was extremely unlikely.  And the competitors had by the late forties and early fifties
developed better specific theories in support of
their traditions.[45]  Thus, at least given my
assumption concerning the problem-solving effectiveness of the competing theories, this partial
study supports thesis 2.

Thesis 3 is the positive aspect of Laudan's
analysis of theory choice.  A scientific community
should accept, or at least hold as the best, that
tradition among a set of competing traditions which
has the greatest problem-solving effectiveness.  I
think this exploratory case study fails to support
thesis 3.  As a matter of fact, Hess' version of
DRIFT became the accepted theory and DRIFT the
accepted tradition only after the confirmation of
Vine-Matthews and Wilson.  Hess' theory was not
even accepted by most oceanographers at Lamont,
Scripps and elsewhere, who were working on similar
problems prior to the corroboration of Vine-
Matthews and Wilson.  Laudan must maintain that
Hess' version of DRIFT only became decidedly
superior in problem-solving effectiveness compared
to competing theories only after the confirmatory
work on Vine-Matthews and Wilson.  However, in

Laudan's terms the confirmation of Vine-Matthews
and Wilson added only two or three more solved
problems to the list of problems solved by Hess'
DRIFT.  Given the healthy increment in the number
of solved empirical problems for the DRIFT tradition with the development of Hess' version, the
addition of two or three more solutions is insufficient to turn the scale decidedly in favor of
DRIFT. If Hess was overwhelmingly accepted after
confirmation of the two hypotheses, the want of
two or three less problems should not have prevented it from having been accepted prior to the
confirmatory work.  Especially since the accepta-
bility to non-acceptability ratio of concerned
oceanographers went up so quickly and significantly.

Laudan may well respond that there was a
difference in the importance of the problems
solved by Vine-Matthews and Wilson than solved by
Hess without the other two hypothese, and that
since they both were extremely weighty problems,
their addition alone was sufficient to tip the
scales. Indeed, Laudan is adamant in his insis-
tence that it isn't only the number of solved
problems which is relevant to questions of theory
choice.  However, none of the criteria he suggests
for evaluating the relative importance of solved
empirical problems is applicable in this case
since none of them allows for distinguishing the
problems solved by Hess from those solved by the
other hypotheses.[46]  The problems solved by the
two hypotheses (cf., why earthquake epicenters have
such-and-such an arrangement at the trenches and
ridges or why there are strips of alternately
polarized seafloor extending symmetrically outward
from ridges) are no more anomaly-producing for competing theories or traditions, no more basic or
archetypal, and no more general than the problems
solved by Hess (cf. how new seafloor is created,
why the seafloor is so young, why the seafloor
gets colder as it gets further away from the
ridges, etc.)  In fact, Vine, Matthews and Wilson
looked at their work as dependent on Hess' seafloor
spreading.

There is a difference between the problems
solved by Vine-Matthews and Wilson and those
solved by Hess, which, although not presently in
Laudan's system, may be added since the difference

is one which is in the spirit of Laudan's stress on problem-solving effectiveness as the criterion for theory choice. The difference concerns the fact that in the cases of Vine-Matthews and Wilson there was the prediction of novel facts, while in Hess' case no novel facts were predicted.[47]

The problems which Vine-Matthews and Wilson solved were not more impressive because of their subject matter; rather they were more impressive because they anticipated and solved a problem before their solved problem became a known problem. In Hess' case, all his solved problems were concerned with answering questions which were already being asked. Hess only solved problems, he did not anticipate the ones which he solved. In general, I am suggesting that a solved empirical problem is inflated in value if it is proposed and solved before or independently of knowing whether the state of affairs giving rise to the problem is real. What could more demonstrate the ability of a theory to solve problems than solving them before they become problematic? Not only can the theory or tradition solve problems after they arise, it can foresee the problematic before it becomes a problem. In addition, usually when a theory or tradition solves an anticipated problem, and correctly anticipates the problem, it is an instant anomaly for competing theories and traditions once existence of the situation giving rise to the problem is confirmed. Vine and Matthews predicted that bands of alternatively polarized material should be found extending symmetrically outward from mid-ocean ridges, and offered seafloor spreading as an answer to why the bands will form in such a manner. Similarly, Wilson predicted that the fault systems along mid-ocean ridges and at trenches should be transform rather than transcurrent, if seafloor was to be created at the ridges and destroyed at the trenches. What they showed once their hypotheses were confirmed was that Hess' version of DRIFT was such an effective problem-solver that it could anticipate and solve problems, let alone merely solve them, and that sufficiently raised the problem-solving ability of Hess' version of DRIFT so that it was decidedly superior to any of the competing theories. Consequently, I suggest that with this addition to Laudan, the conclusion of this exploratory study is that his analysis can explain the seemingly irrational behavior of the geological community not to accept some form of DRIFT for over fifty years as eminently rational, and that Laudan's analysis when appended with a distinction between anticipating solutions and non-anticipating solutions fits the development and reception of DRIFT.

## References

[1]Larry Laudan, Progress and Its Problems: Towards a Theory of Scientific Growth (Berkeley, 1977).

[2]Ibid., 79.

[3]Ibid., 15.

[4]Ibid., 18.

[5]Ibid., 19.

[6]Ibid., 22.

[7]Ibid., 27.

[8]Ibid., 22.

[9]Ibid., 35.

[10]Laudan also suggests criteria for weighting the relative importance of solved problems with one another and anomalous problems with one another. However, I shall not discuss this aspect of his taxonomy until Section III where it becomes relevant.

[11]Ibid., 47.

[12]Ibid., 49.

[13]Ibid., 53.

[14]All quotations in this essay by Wegener (unless specified otherwise) are from the Dover 1966 English edition of Die Entstehung der

Kontinente und Ozeanne.  This Dover edition is a new English translation of the 1962 printing of the fourth revised edition of The Origin of Continents and Oceans published in 1929 by Friedr. Vieweg and Son.

[15]Ibid., 76-77.

[16]Ibid., 20.

[17]Ibid., 17.

[18]Ibid., 175.

[19]Ibid., 167.

[20]P. Lake, "Wegener's Displacement Theory," Geological Magazine, 1922, 50:338-346 (339).

[21]Ibid., 339.

[22]H. Jeffreys, The Earth (London, 1924), 261. Moreover, I believe that this third part of the mechanisms objection was more empirical than conceptual.  Here Jeffreys and other argued that since seafloor material (basalt) is stronger than continental material (granite), the continents would be unable to survive horizontal displacement.  Here the clash was between Wegener's claim that the continents have displaced themselves horizontally and the general fact that seafloor material was stronger or more rigid than continental material. In addition, it was not the case that proponents of competing theories had a solution to the problem of why the continents are made up of weaker material than the seafloor; they did not have a solution.  But, the fact that continental material is weaker than seafloor material was not a problem for them.  Thus, Wegener's DRIFT had an additional mechanistic problem which was both unshared by the competition and was really empirical in nature. This leads me to suspect that an addition has to be made to Laudan's taxonomy of empirical problems, namely empirical problems which are unsolved and unshared.  These problems count more heavily against a theory than the typical unsolved problem since they do a double disservice to a

theory possessed with one.  Not only is the theory
faced with a recognized unsolved empirical problem,
but the problem is an empirical problem which its
rivals don't have to consider.

[23]W. D. Wright, "The Wegenerian Hypothesis,"
Nature, 1923, 111:30-31 (31).

[24]This 1926 symposium was the first inter-
national symposium on continental drift.

[25]W. Van Waterschoot van der Gracht (ed.),
Theory of Continental Drift: A Symposium on the
Origin and Movement of Land Masses both Inter-
continental and Intra-continental, as Proposed by
Alfred Wegener (Tulsa, 1928), 119-120.  Besides
editing the selections from the 1926 symposium
for publication in 1928, van der Gracht included
two papers of his own.

[26]Wegener (note 14) 60.

[27]Joly began investigating the interplay
between radioactivity and geology as early as 1908.
Cf., J. Joly, "Uranium and Geology," Annual Report
of the Smithsonian Institution 1908, 355-384.
His 1923 version of DRIFT appeared in an article,
"The Movements of the Earth's Surface Crust,"
Philosophical Magazine, 45:1167-1188.

[28]Alex Du Toit, Our Wandering Continents
(London, 1937).

[29]A. Holmes, "Some Problems of Physical
Geology and the Earth's Thermal History," Geological Magazine, 1927, 64:263-278.

[30]H. Jeffreys in "Problems of the Earth's
Crust: A discussion in Section E (Geography) of
the British Association on 28 September 1931 in
the Hall of the Society," Geological Journal, 1931,
78:433-455 (453).

[31]An excellent account of the whole episode
may be found in Longwell,"My Estimate of Continental Drift Concept," in W. Carey (ed.),

*Continental Drift: A Symposium on the Present Status of the Continental Drift Hypothesis, held in the Geology Department of the University* of Tasmania, 1-12. This symposium was one of the first major meetings after World War II on DRIFT, and it had two major advocates of DRIFT, viz., Carey and King.

[32]Hess did not publish his thesis until 1962, while Dietz published his version of seafloor spreading in 1961. However, Hess deserves credit for he distributed an unpublished version of his thesis in 1960. Thanks to Professor Sheldon Judson, Chairman, Department of Geological and Geophysical Sciences, Princeton University, I have had the opportunity to examine the 1960 version. There are no substantial changes between the two versions. In addition, Dietz has freely admitted that Hess first developed the notion of "seafloor spreading."

> As regards sea-floor spreading, Hess deserves full credit for the concept. . . .
> I have done little more than introduce the term sea-floor spreading. . . .

From R. S. Dietz, "Reply," *Jounal of Geophysical Research*, 73:6567. Dietz's 1961 article on DRIFT appeared as "Continent and Ocean Basin Evolution by Spreading of the Sea Floor," *Nature*, 190:854-857, and Hess' 1962 version appeared as "History of Ocean Basins," in *Petrologic Studies: A Volume to Honor A. F. Buddington*, 599-620.

[33]Hess (note 32), (1960), 32-3, and (1962), 618.

[34]Hess (note 32), (1960), 14-5, and (1962), 608.

[35]Hess (note 32), (1962), 608-609 and with slight alteration, Hess (1960), 16.

[36]F. Vine and D. Matthews, "Magnetic Anomalies over Oceanic Ridges," *Nature,* 1961, 199:947-949 (948).

[36]J. Heirtzler and X. le Pichon, "Crustal Structure of the Mid-Ocean Ridges," *Journal of*

Geophysical Research, 1965, 70:4013-4033 (4028).

[38]See, for example, F. Vine, "Spreading of the Ocean Floor: New Evidence," Science, 1966, 154: 1405-1415.

[39]W. Wertenbaker, The Floor of the Sea (Boston, 1974), 203-205.

[40]T. Wilson, "A New Class of Faults and Their Bearing on Continental Drift," Nature, 207:343-347 (343).

[41]Ibid., 344.

[42]B. Isacks, J. Oliver and L. Sukes, "Seismology and the New Global Tectonics," Journal of Geophysical Research, 1968, 73:5855-5899 (5860).

[43]I have recently applied the account of scientific growth and change as put forth by the late Imre Lakatos to the career of DRIFT. For reasons beyond the scope of this paper I think, even given the exploratory nature of this piece that Laudan's account provides a better "fit." However, a more extensive analysis of Laudan wherein explicit comparison of Lakatos is required to settle the issues. Cf., H. Frankel, "The Career of Continental Drift Theory: An Application of Imre Lakatos' analysis of scientific growth to the rise of drift theory," forthcoming. Studies in History and Philosophy of Science. An earlier version of the Lakatos paper was presented at the New Hampshire Bicentennial Conference on the History of Geology, and a section of the earlier version dealing with the importance of seafloor spreading will appear in the Proceedings. H. Frankel, "Why Drift Theory was accepted with the confirmation of Harry Hess' concept of seafloor spreading."

[44]Actually, Laudan in his section wherein he gives criteria for the relative weighting of conceptual problems (cf., 64-66) does not include the centrality of a conceptual problem to the theory or tradition for which the given problem is a problem as a relevant consideration. However, I should

like to suggest that the weight of a conceptual
problem is greater for a theory if the elements
which are in tension are used in the solution to
many of the solved empirical problems, the point
being that the harder it is to exorcise those
elements of a theory bringing about the conceptual
problem, the more difficult it is to formulate new
versions of the theory or traditions not containing the elements giving rise to the problem, and
the more important it is to remove the elements.

[45]Although for the purposes of this paper I
have spoken of the relative success of theories
and traditions which competed with DRIFT in the
fifties in accounting for somewhat similar problems
as an assumption, I should like to give a hint of
how I would start to support the assumption if I
were to offer support.  A tradition which competed
with DRIFT was permanentism.  Permanentists believed
that for the most part continents and ocean basins
had remained in their present positions since forming, although they did allow for the growth of continents through time.  They argued that the present
continents had increased in size by extending outward from original continental landmasses called
nuclei or cratons.  Alan H. Voisey, then a geologist at the University of New England in Armidale,
New South Wales, summarised this accretionist position rather nicely in a paper he delivered at the
1956 symposium on continental drift organized by
Warren Carey at the University of Tasmania.  This
summary is especially interesting since Voisey explicitly points out that he thinks the problem
solving ability of this accretion theory is greater
than that of DRIFT.

> Poldervaart (1955, 137-141) submitted his
> views on the origin of continental nuclei
> referring also the views of Wilson (1949),
> Bucher (1950), Kay (1951) and Rubey (1953).
> The present writer also subscribes to the
> general principles of continental growth put
> forward by these workers, which involve the
> formation of geosynclines around continental
> nuclei, the development of island arcs and
> the growth of the continents by a process of
> accretion.  He also believes in the continuity
> of geological processes. . . . While these
> concepts are not necessarily incompatible
> with some form of continental drift they
> provide alternative solutions to some of the

problems which it has been claimed to
solve.
Voisey then goes on to argue for the accretion hypothesis over that of drift, and concludes with the
following:

In the opinion of the writer continental
drift does not now appear to be as unlikely from the geophysical viewpoint
as was thought twenty years ago.  On the
other hand, the biological arguments
favouring it seem to have weakened and
alternative hypotheses have gained strength.
Cf., Alan H. Voisey, "Some Comments on the hypothesis of continental drift," in S. W. Carey, con-
vener, Continental Drift--A Symposium (1958,
Hobart), 162-171.  The first of the above quotations is from pp. 162-163, and the second one is
from p. 169.

[46]Laudan suggests the following means by which
a solved empirical problem may increase in importance: Problem inflation by solution--here a
problem is inflated once a solution is offered.
This is essentially Laudan's point that most unsolved problems don't really become problems
until solved.  Problem inflation by anomaly solu-
tion--here a solution to an anomaly is considered
to have more weight than a solution to an unsolved
problem.  Problem inflation by archetype construc-
tion--those solved empirical problems which employ
the use of techniques used in many of the other
solutions offered by the theory or refer to basic
processes to which other processes in the theory
or tradition are reduced, are considered more important than solutions which do not utilize such
techniques or refer to such processes.  Problem
weighting by generality--here the more general the
problem solved the more important the problem.
None of these criteria differentiates between the
problems solved by Vine-Matthews or Wilson from
those solved by Hess.

[47]Students of scientific methodology will recognize that this distinction I am drawing has
been developed most recently by the late Imre Lakatos.  There are, however, problems with his account
which, I believe, can be avoided by its being put
in terms of 'solved problems' rather than 'explained facts' and by not requiring that whenever

a theory supercedes a competing theory it must predict novel facts.   I am only suggesting that there
are times when the problem-solving effectiveness
of a theory is greatly enhanced by its ability to
anticipate empirical problems in addition to merely
solving empirical problems.

# 3

# Reception of Acupuncture by the Scientific Community

## From Scorn to a Degree of Interest

John Z. Bowers

Acupuncture has been described as a hypnotic maneuver, an Oriental trick, or just plain trash! It is, however, one of the most widely practiced and popular methods of Chung-i, Chinese traditional medicine, which is still followed to some extent not only in China, but in other countries influenced by Chinese culture--Japan, Malaysia, Singapore, Indo-China, Korea, and Taiwan. In addition, more than twenty million overseas Chinese cling to aspects of their ancient medicine. Thus the total following approximates up to one-third of the world's people.

Essentially, acupuncture is the insertion of solid needles into specific points of the skin. It is based on the Ching-lo system in which the skin points are thought to be connected to twelve channels or meridians, each of which in turn is believed to terminate in a major organ. Thus there is a liver meridian, a kidney meridian, and so forth. Only the brain, which is considered inviolate, is not represented by a meridian. The Ching-lo system has never been identified anatomically.

The origins of acupuncutre may go back as far as the first of the three dynasties: the Hsia, circa--2200 B.C. to 1760 B.C. Some of the earliest needles were chipped from stone, suggesting that acupuncture was practiced in the Neolithic periods. Beginning with the Han dynasty, 202 B.C. to 220 A.D., the procedure grew steadily in popularity and prestige. The Imperial Medical College of the opulent T'ang Dynasty, 618 A.D. to 906 A.D., included acupuncture among its six professorial

chairs.  Treatises extolling the glories of the
procedure were prepared under Imperial rescript.

It is germane that China and its medicine remained isolated from the revolutionary development
in medical science that began at Padua in the six-
teenth century.  Responsible for this isolation
was the Chinese conviction that Cathay was "The
Middle Kingdom," surrounded by a primitive world
that had nothing to contribute to its cultural
supremacy.  When the first Europeans, the Portu-
guese, appeared off the Cantonese coast in 1514,
they were termed Namban, southern barbarians and
when George III sought to establish diplomatic
and commercial intercourse with the Son of Heaven
at Peking in the middle of the eighteenth century,
he was singularly rebuffed.  "As to your entreaty
to send one of your nationals to be accredited to
my Celestial Court and to be in control of your
country's trade with China, this request is contrary to the usage of my dynasty and cannot possibly be entertained. . . . Swaying the wide world,
I have but one aim in view, namely to maintain a
perfect governance and to fulfill the duties of
the State. . . . I set no values on objects strange
or ingenious and have no use for your country's
manufactures," wrote Emperor Ch'un Lung, who ruled
1735 to 1795 A.D.[1]

The cultural veneration of the human body as
a sacred treasure that could not be violated was
a second reason for the lack of change in Chinese
medicine.  Thus it was not until 1913, more than
three and a half centuries after Andreas Vesalius
introduced modern anatomy in his great work, De
Humani Corporis Fabrica, 1543, that the first
autopsy was permitted in China.  Permission was
granted when the need to learn from western medical
science became apparent during a devastating epi-
demic of pneumonic plague that took 60,000 lives
in Manchuria.

## The Western View

The exotic practice of acupuncture fascinated
the first western physicians who came to the Orient.
Their vantage point was Dejima, the small Dutch
trading post established in 1641 at Nagasaki.  A
large Chinese colony where acupuncture was practiced adjoined Dejima, and numerous Japanese

acupuncturists walked the lanes of Nagasaki huck-
stering their art. The first description of acupuncture by a western physician, Willem Ten Rhijne's
Dissertatio de Arthritide, was published in 1683.
Ten Rhijne reported that acupuncture was useful
for "headache, vertigo, cataracts, apoplexy, stiff
neck, nervous convulsions, epilepsy, catarrh and
rheumatism, melancholia, intestinal worms, diarrhea
and dysentery, cholera, but above all, for colic
pain and other intestinal ailments produced by
winds, spontaneous weakness also created by winds,
swelling of the testicles, arthritis, and lastly
gonorrhea."[2]

The records on the reception of acupuncture
in most countries of western Europe are fragmen-
tary. The technique may have become known in
Russia as early as the first contacts with China
during the early Ming Dynasty, 1368-1644 A.D.
After the treaty of Nerchinsk, 1689, which was the
first between China and Russia, a Russian medical
mission visited China to study inoculation against
smallpox. They observed other medical practices
and were, in part, responsible for a degree of
interest in acupuncture in Russia.

Lorenz Heister (1683-1758), the outstanding
German surgeon of his period, discussed the use of
acupuncture in his Chirurgie, 1758, which was
translated into six languages in some twenty print-
ings. It was a vehicle for the dissemination of
knowledge of the technique in western Europe.

Acupuncture gained its greatest popularity in
France. It was used by leaders of French medicine
in the early decades of the nineteenth century,
when Paris was the world center of medicine. Students from other European countries and from
America and Latin America flocked to the great
teaching hospitals, Hotel Dieu and Le Charité, of
Paris and must have observed the practice of acupuncture.

After the conquest of Indo-China in 1862, acupuncture gained in status and a major surge of
interest began in 1927. In that year, Georges
Soulie de Morant, who had become an acupuncture
master during twenty years as French Consul in
Shanghai, returned to Paris and popularized the
technique by practicing, teaching, and writing
about it.

Edward Jukes, accoucheur and surgeon of London, is reported to have introduced acupuncture in England on February 18, 1821, when he treated a patient for continuing pains in the thighs. Sir William MacEwen (1848-1924), Professor of Surgery at the University of Glasgow, used acupuncture in the treatment of aortic aneurysm.

In America, two of our most distinguished physicians tested acupuncture, Silar Weir Mitchell (1829-1914), the leading American neurologist of his period, probably became familiar with acupuncture when he studied in Paris, 1852. In his first description of causalgia, Mitchell states that he found acupuncture ineffectual in its treatment.

It may come as a shock to the American medical profession, which sneers at acupuncture, to know that our most revered physician, Sir William Osler, recommended the technique for the treatment of sciatica and lumbago in his famed Textbook of Medicine. An amusing incident concerns Osler's effort to cure a wealthy Montreal sugar refiner who suffered from intractable lumbago. Osler had anticipated that by curing the sugar magnate he would gain a major benefaction for McGill, where he was Professor of Medicine. But the patient swore loudly with each jab of a needle, and finally hobbled from Osler's office in disgust. Osler bemoaned his lack of success, which he claimed might have "meant a million for McGill."[3]

In Europe today, there is widespread interest in acupuncture, and it is practiced by a significant number of physicians. In France, the technique is officially recognized by the Académie de Médecine, and there are over 700 medical graduates practicing it. In other European countries, although it is practiced by physicians, acupuncture has not achieved the same degree of professional acceptance as in France.

There was no effort in Europe to study the mechanism of acupuncture. The handful of experimental physiologist in Europe in the first half of the nineteenth century were more concerned with the physiology of the human body than with an exotic and questionable practice. Further, research in neurophysiology did not ripen until the ascendancy

of the English school of physiologists at the end
of the century.

On three distinct occasions the western scientific community exhibited its apathy to acupuncture.  The first was when the German medical mission arrived in Tokyo in the 1870s to found the
Faculty of Medicine of Tokyo Imperial University.
A major responsibility of the German mission was
to prepare Japanese to be their successors, and
after graduation, the most promising students
were sent to Germany for extended training in basic
research.  Although they were well aware of the
popularity of acupuncture, and had been trained in
research-dominated faculties of medicine, the
Germans spurned the method.  An indication of their
attitude is that while they wrote prolifically
about the diseases and anthropology of Japan, I
have been unable to find any communication about
acupuncture.

The Japanese scientists who succeeded the
German took a similar approach.  This latter attitude deserves a special note, since their singular
affection for research on the nervous system and
brain, could easily have led them to studies of
the procedure.  Further, most of them had probably
received acupuncture.

A second western confrontation with acupuncture came with the founding in 1911 of the Japan-
ese-sponsored South Manchuria Medical College at
Mukden, where a large Japanese community was employed by the Japanese-owned South Manchuria Rail-
way.  A major purpose of the school was to deal
with the medical problems of China.  It attracted
some of the best academics from Japan, most of
whom had trained in research in the leading laboratories of Germany and Britain.  Their studies
at Mukden ranged from malnutrition to the pioneer-
ing investigations of the physiology of perspira-
tion.  But the archives of the school do not
mention acupuncture.

A third and most significant example of the
attitude of the scientific community was that of
the faculty of the renowned Peking Union Medical
College (PUMC), which in its heyday, 1921-41, was
the Johns Hopkins of China.  PUMC's major

objectives were: "1. To give a medical education comparable to that provided by the best medical schools of the United States and Europe; and 2. To afford opportunities for research, especially with reference to problems peculiar to the Orient."[4] With this charge a number of the brilliant faculty at PUMC who were drawn from our best medical schools, turned their research efforts to China's varied and exotic diseases that were then rampant. Davidson Black of the Anatomy Department uncovered the skeleton of Peking Man; K. K. Chen and Carl Schmidt introduced the use of ephedrine, a potent sympathomimetic agent. They isolated it from an indigenous medicine, Ma Huang, which Chen obtained from a Chinese herbalist who was using it to treat Chen's mother for asthma.

Since physiological studies were appropriate for the investigation of acupuncture, it is of special interest that Robert K. S. Lim, an Amoy Chinese and leader of the Physiology Department, had trained in neurophysiology with E. A. Sharpey-Schafer, the distinguished Edingurgh scientist. Lim had observed acupuncturists over a number of years, but shunned the practice as did other members of the PUMC faculty.

Until the 1950s, then, only a few members of the scientific community were aware of acupuncture and the attitude of the faculties at Tokyo, Mukden, and Peking exemplified that of other scientists who were familiar with the technique--they scorned it as no better than quackery and would not deign to investigate a possible mechanism for its effectiveness.

## Revolutionary Applications

When Mao Tse-tung and his victorious Communist party gained power they moved vigorously to restore the eminence of Chinese traditional medicine and to use the best of western medicine with the traditional. Acupuncture became the focal point and its curative powers in asthma, hypertension, pneumonia and acute appendicitis were proclaimed in Chinese medical journals and propaganda leaflets. Further emphasis on the technique came with The Great Leap Forward in 1958, and claims for its therapeutic effectiveness included infectious diseases, gastro-intestinal diseases and skin

disorders.  It appeared that acupuncture could cure
or ameliorate every ailment.

## Onset of Current Western Interest

A principal factor in the surge of interest in
Chinese medicine goes back to the visit of President Richard M. Nixon in 1972.  Acupuncture gained
new currency during that visit when James B. Reston
the distinguished journalist required an emergency
appendectomy.  He suffered postoperative disten-
tion, which was said to have been relieved drama-
tically by acupuncture.  This was heralded in the
Western media, and some of the stories were garbled
so that many readers concluded that Reston's appendectomy had been performed under acupuncture anesthesia.

The historic fixation of Americans on China
was rekindled and we moved enthusiastically to
build relationships.  Other nations followed suit.
In those years the wonders of Chinese medicine--
acupuncture, barefoot doctors, eradication of snail
fever (schistosomiasis) were leading propaganda
pieces for the Chinese.  Thus it was only natural
that Western physicians were constrained to take a
new look at medical practices in China rather than
scorning them.  And, many of these were men and
women who had not been steeped in the earlier
scornful attitudes.

## Acupuncture for Deaf Mutes

By 1965, Chinese publications told of striking
successes in the treatment of children who had
neurosensory deafness.  The needles were inserted
at the dangerous ya men point, near the base of
the skull, and in the preauricular regions.  The
period of treatment extended from one to four
years, and was supplemented by special schools in
which the children were taught lip-reading and
phonation.  (At that time, I attributed any claims
of success to the excellent and dedicated instruc-
tion in these schools.)

Samuel Rosen, M.D., a distinguished otolaryngologist, visited China in 1973 and observed the
treatment of deaf mutes.  On his return, his pilot
study of forty children: "failed to reveal any

consistently maintained improvement."[5]   In addition, Rosen noted that the Chinese reports were not
based on audiometric studies, but were impression-
istic.   Others gave negative reports and decried
the proliferation of acupuncture clinics for deafness in the United States.   One otolaryngologist
commented that the soaring popularity of acupuncture for deafness was attributable in part to the
inclination of American otolaryngologists to:
"abandon our sensorineural hearing loss patients."[6]

In a personal communication, however, Dr.
Rosen informed me that he is now testing acupuncture therapy in patients who have retained a
slight degree of hearing--his earlier study was on
children who had no measurable hearing and were
treated for only six months.   The Chinese are now
evaluating acupuncture therapy in sensorineural
deafness more objectively.   It is clear that the
early figures citing remarkable successes were
exaggerated, and were not based on objective
measurements.   At the same time, the Chinese continue to work assiduously with acupuncture in the
treatment of nerve deafness.   A recent verbal report to Dr. Rosen from China states that "very
marked improvement is achieved in about eight
percent of the patients and some improvement in
eleven percent.   Objective audiometry is now being
carried on, as well as research in the methodology."

## Acupuncture Analgesia

Since  acupuncture has been used for many years
in the treatment of pain, Chinese physicians
reasoned that it could also be effective as an
anesthetic agent.   After its first use in 1958,
it soon became the leading source of propagandizing
the "new" medicine in China.   Surgical procedures
under acupuncture anesthesia became the star attrac-
tion for visiting delegations.   They viewed major
operations on the neck, thorax, and abdomen in
which acupuncture was said to be the sole anesthetic agent.   Patients were not only conscious and
communicative, but some even stepped from the operating table without assistance at the end of the procedure to express their gratitude to the surgical
team--and to the ever-present portrait of Mao Tse-
tung.

The rationale proposed by the Peking Acupunctural Anesthesia Coordinating Group in 1972 was not acceptable to the scientific community.[7] Teich'i is said to suppress sensory pain stimuli at the level of the brain and to enable the patient to maintain normal respiratory and circulatory physiology during surgery.

The early reports stated that acupuncture anesthesia was effective in ninety percent of the cases. However, in 1973, a visiting medical delegation representing the National Academy of Sciences was told that its use had 'leveled off,' and estimated that it was being used in no more than six to seven percent of all surgical cases.[8] The report expressed disappointment that there had been virtually no clinical research on acupuncture anesthesia. It concluded, however: "There is no doubt that acupuncture analgesia is effective in permitting operations in certain highly selected patients."[9]

## Acupuncture in Drug Abuse

With mounting disillusion about existing modalities for treating drug abuse, interest has risen in the validity of non-pharmacological approaches-- hypnosis, bio-feedback, transcendental meditation and, not surprisingly, acupuncture. Acupuncture therapy for heroin and opium addicts was first tried in 1972 in Hong Kong, where the procedure is widely practiced and drug addiction is a major problem.[10] The technique in treating addiction is to insert acupuncture needles into the "lung" points of the ear and to apply an electro-stimulator for about thirty minutes. Laboratory experiments using acupuncture on addicted rats have resulted in attenuation of withdrawal symptoms.[11]

Preliminary follow-up studies in humans suggest that the patients probably lose their addiction for a longer period than do those on methadone. Thus far there has been no satisfactory explanation of the mechanism of acupuncture therapy. If acupuncture stimulates the production of endorphins as preliminary studies suggest, their morphine-like effect might explain a role for acupuncture in the treatment of opiate addiction.

## Mechanisms

Successful attempts at acupuncture anesthesia have been ascribed to psychic phenomena relating to hypnosis. However, studies from China suggest that a humoral factor may be significant. One study reports that in cross-circulation experiments between an acupunctured and a control rabbit, the pain threshold of the control animal was elevated. Another states that spinal fluid withdrawn from an animal under acupuncture produces analgesia in a second animal. Dr. Tsung O. Cheng, Professor of Medicine at Georgetown University Medical School and an observer of China, speculates that current evidence indicates that acupuncture is eighty-five percent psychic and fifteen percent humoral.[12]

## Neurobiological Studies

A major barrier to elucidating acupuncture analgesia is our poor understanding of the mechanism of pain. However, the surge of pain research in the neurosciences may resolve the question of a physiological basis for the procedure. The pioneer studies in 1965, by Patrick D. Wall and Ronald Melzack, on the "spinalgate" theory of pain, which they subsequently revised, were evaluated in relation to acupuncture. One aspect of the gate-theory was that certain afferent stimuli abolish pain by inhibition of the spinal cells that relate to the region in which pain stimuli are generated. Wall now points out that this explanation is invalid since there is no anatomical correlation between the site of the operation and the points in which the acupuncture needles are inserted.[13] For example, pelvic surgery is carried out with needles inserted into points on the forearm.

The second aspect of the gate-theory was that "descending controls from the brain may inhibit the transmission of pain-producing impulses."[14] Wall finds this explanation to be premature since the mechanism of such descending controls has not been elucidated.

## Endorphins and Acupuncture

The focus of scientific interest has shifted to endorphins--literally, "the morphine within."

Endorphins, a part of the body's natural mechanisms for dealing with pain, are produced in the brain and most copiously in the pituitary gland. It is possible that needles stimulate the secretion of the opiate-like endorphins and have the same effect as the injection of a narcotic. Professor C. H. Li has developed a highly sensitive and specific radioimmunoassay for humans which should verify or negate this proposal.

Bruce Pomeranz, M.D., Ph.D., Associate Professor of Neurobiology at the University of Toronto, has recorded electric potential of single cells in the spinal cord of anesthetized animals and found that acupuncture diminished the responses. He reports that after removal of the pituitary gland, acupuncture had no effect. Pomeranz proposes that this supports the theory that acupuncture stimulates the production of endorphins for which the pituitary, as we have noted, is the principal reservoir.

Naloxone, a specific morphine antagonist which blocks the effect of endorphins, also blocks the effects of acupuncture. Thus it is possible that acupuncture may produce a pain-killing effect by increasing the release of Beta-endorphins or by affecting the same receptors in the brain as opiates.

Patrick D. Wall prefers the studies of M. Eriksson and B. Sjolund, Department of Clinical Physiology, University of Lund.[15] They have shown that intermittent electrical stimulation within the segment of pain, produces relief in about thirty percent of patients and term this 'acupuncture-like electroanalgesia.' It is associated with a local release of endorphin from the stimulated segments and the therapeutic relief is reversed by naloxone. Studies by D. J. Mayer and D. D. Price at the Medical College of Virginia, confirm the naloxone reversal.

## Adrenal Corticotrophic Hormone

Professor Ma Lin, Department of Biochemistry at The Chinese University of Hong Kong, has found that acupuncture stimulates the excretion of ACTH in rats.[16]

## Psychic Factors

No matter how valid the theories on endorphins as a neurobiochemical base for acupuncture may prove to be, the significance of psychic factors cannot be denied. One consideration, which we have noted, may be the stoicism of the Chinese. American surgeons who worked at the Peking Union Medical College believe it is this quality that allowed operations that would have required general anesthesia in the United States, to be performed under local and regional anesthesia.[17]

Another factor is faith, unswerving faith in a practice that has been an inherent part of the Chinese tradition for several millenia. Today children are indoctrinated in acupuncture during special after-school activities. They trace the meridians and points on outlines of human figures and insert needles into stuffed socks and each other. In turn, they teach other children. "Faith and knowledge lean heavily upon each other in the practice of medicine."[18]

In addition, the needles may serve to distract the patient from pain. This effect is enhanced for surgical procedures by the application of a mechanical vibrator that oscillates the needles several hundred times a minute. The effect is further heightened by the attachment of a six-volt current at about 100 cycles per second. Each pulse produces a twitch in the muscle, giving an added motion to the needle.

Another context in which acupuncture must be seen is the close and continuing interaction between the practitioner and patient that has been a cardinal feature of Chinese medicine through the centuries. The training of patients for acupuncture anesthesia often begins two weeks before an operation. This contrasts sharply with the hustle-bustle style of too many physicians in the west.

## Conclusions

As we have seen, acupuncture was shunned for many decades by the scientific community. The introduction of acupuncture anesthesia, which proved successful in a small percentage of patients,

awakened a limited interest. The advances in research in neurobiology have opened new opportunities to understand the poorly understood mechanisms of pain. We need to initiate psychophysical
as well as neurobiological studies on acupuncture
to elucidate any links between the manifest psychic factors and the increasingly probable organic
contributions.

Patrick Wall commented recently: "Acupuncture
is a fact and a very startling one. It is used on
a minority of people in some operations. The
Chinese have shown just how powerful and how
limited this method is. We should try to improve
the method. That will not be done by adding to
the mythology but by exploring the nature of the
factors involved."[19]

## References

[1] Quoted in A. J. Toynbee, Civilization on
Trial (Oxford, 1948), 72.

[2] Willem Ten Rhijne, Dissertatio de arthritide:
mantissa schematica de acupunctura et orationes
tres de chymiae et botaniae antiquitate et digni-
tate, de physionomia et de monstris (London, The
Hague, Leipzig, 1683), 186.

[3] H. Cushing, The Life of Sir William Osler,
2 vols. (Oxford, 1925), I, 177.

[4] Statement by Franklin J. McLean, quoted in
J. Z. Bowers, Western Medicine in a Chinese
Palace" Peking Union Medical College, 1917-1951
(Josiah Macy, Jr. Foundation, New York, 1972), 68.

[5] S. Rosen, "Feasibility of Acupuncture as a
Treatment for Sensory-Neural Deafness in Children,"
The Laryngoscope, 1974, 84:2202.

[6] Ibid., 2215

[7] Peking Acupunctural Anaesthesia Cooperation
and Coordination Group, "The Principle of Acupunctural Anaesthesia," Peking Review, 1972, 15:17-20.

[8]*Report of the Medical Delegation to the People's Republic of China*. June 15 to July 6, 1973, National Academy of Sciences, Institute of Medicine, Washington, D. C.

[9]*Ibid.*, 79.

[10]H. L. Wen and S. Y. Cheung, "Treatment of Drug Addiction by Acupuncture and Electrical Stimulation," *American Journal of Acupuncture*, 1973, 1:71-75.

[11]L. K. Ng, unpublished report. Referred to in P. G. Bourne, "Non-pharmocological Approaches to the Treatment of Drug Abuse," *American Journal of Chinese Medicine*, 1975, 3:235-244.

[12]Personal communication, 1977.

[13]P. D. Wall, "The Gate Control Theory of Pain Mechanisms: A Critique of a Critical Review." Undated and unpublished communication.

[14]*Ibid.*

[15]Personal communication, 1978.

[16]Personal communication.

[17]Personal communication, H. Loucks, 1970.

[18]Peter Mere Latham (1798-1875), *The Collected Works of Dr. P. M. Latham*, 2 vols. (London, 1876-1878), II, 408.

[19]*Two Eyes on a Needle*, Patrick D. Wall, Confidential Report to the Medical Research Council, London, undated, 12.

# 4

# The Controversy Over Statistics in Parapsychology 1934 - 1938

Seymour H. Mauskopf and Michael R. McVaugh

In modern times, the most significant bid for the academic normalization of parapsychology occurred in the decade of the 1930's and was associated with the first work of J. B. Rhine at Duke University. Rhine claimed to have demonstrated human psychic abilities not by calling forth dramatic psychic phenomena but by utilizing an experimental card guessing technique and analyzing the results statistically. Rhine's work engendered considerable controversy in the 1930's, but by the end of the decade parapsychology had achieved the peripheral acceptance which at best still characterizes the field.

In this paper, we shall discuss the initial response and ensuing debate over Rhine's work, one which focused not on its experimental foundations but on the statistical basis of his claims. Initially, this debate took place between the parapsychologists (really Rhine and his small group at Duke) and a few psychologists, but it came to involve mathematicians and statisticians as well. What we shall try to show in this account is that the perception of parapsychology as "unconventional" in these first years was hardly a simple or an absolute perception. In particular, the protagonist psychologists and mathematicians had very different perspectives on how--and indeed whether--Rhine's work was unconventional.

The research for this paper was supported in part by a National Science Foundation research grant, 73-05467.

Psychical research, the investigation of super-normal phenomena and abilities, was first organized in the 1880's with the founding of the S.P.R. in London in 1882 and the A.S.P.R. in the U.S. at the end of 1884. Although spiritualistic interests found a focus in such activities as the collection of accounts of hauntings and the investigations of mediums etc., almost from the beginning it was realized that certain research strategies, if only they could be implemented, would be more likely to further the scientific knowledge of psychic phenomena and convince critical and skeptical outsiders: research into purported human psychic abilities such as telepathy and clairvoyance carried out by the use of simple test materials amenable to statistical treatment, such as playing cards, so as to permit the quantitative assessment of the improbability of the results. During the 1880's, there was a spate of such tests reported by members of the S.P.R., by the French physiologist Charles Richet and--in somewhat more critical tone--by the A.S.P.R. Moreover, the British in particular made serious efforts to get a refined statistical algorithm by which "degree of success" could be evaluated. By the end of the decade, however, nothing very decisive had been reported and interest among psychical researchers became concentrated on more striking--and less experimentally testable and quantifiable--manifestations of spiritualistic phenomena and psychic abilities. There had always been those in the psychical research movement who insisted that even in the case of telepathy it was poor strategy to try to provoke its manifestation by something as utterly mundane as card guessing since, in ordinary life, reports of thought transfer usually accompanied extremely emotional, highly charged situations.

Therefore, after the mid-1890's, experimental testing of psychic abilities by card guessing became at best a sporadic pursuit. It was taken up in this country in the second decade of this century and again in the 1920's in a few universities which had received support for psychical research (Stanford and Harvard) and it was revived in England with no less a statistician than R. A. Fisher serving as an advisor. But the overall results were no more compelling than they had been previously; no ongoing research program was

as a necessary result of the inherent skewness
of the ESP test distribution--a consequence of the
inequality of the values of p and q (1/5 and 4/5).
This skewness, Willoughby asserted, would remain
constant no matter how large the number of trials
to be evaluated became.  While Willoughby raised
other statistical and methodological issues, this
one was his principal focus.[7]

Rhine for his part turned to his assistant
and graduate student, Charles E. Stuart, who had
some competence in mathematics and statistics, to
handle the discussion with Willoughby.  Willoughby
had almost immediately put his arguments into
print and Stuart followed suit with a reply. In his
response, Stuart was able to demonstrate that the
skewness of the ESP guessing curve rapidly grew
smaller as the number of trials increased, becoming
already insignificant at twenty-five trials.[8]
Although the discussions (and articles) between
Willoughby and Stuart carried on into 1936, by
September of that year, Willoughby was willing to
concede that his statistical objections  "won't
hold water."[9]  Willoughby remained puzzled and even
skeptical of Rhine's work, but interested and
open-minded enough to put a student of his own onto
ESP experiments.

By the time of Willoughby's concession, a
more formidable critic of Rhine had appeared in
Chester E. Kellogg, a psychologist at McGill University.  If Willoughby belonged more to the
second of the above mentioned categories of
interest in ESP work--the young psychologist intri-
gued by the claims of Rhine--Kellogg clearly belonged to the first.  He was considerably older
than Willoughby; his acquaintance with psychical
research went back two decades to his days in Hugo
Muensterberg's graduate seminar at Harvard in 1913-
1914.[10]  Kellogg was clearly more concerned about
parapsychology than most psychologists; he was one
of the very few on record to accord Rhine's monograph serious attention when it appeared, having
taken it up in his seminar on contemporary psychology in the academic year, 1934-1935.[11]  But his
interest was an intensely critical one and in this
Kellogg conformed to a traditional attitude among
American psychologists, represented perhaps most
notably by Joseph Jastrow.

Although Kellogg's style of exposition was not very lucid, he did have a deeper understanding of the statistical issues than did Willoughby and he was consequently able to formulate his objections to Rhine's statistical procedures more effectively and more generally. His main point of criticism involved a basic assumption about the ESP test situation implicit in the use of the normal distribution, namely, independence of trials. He pointed out that neither the sequence of cards or guesses were random sequences, nor were they independent of each other. Instead, Rhine's test situation was a case of the matching of two sequences, one of which (the test deck) had a fixed quinquepartite makeup (five each of each symbol) and the other of which (the guesses) was made non-random by factors such as symbol preference, perseveration, expectation, and the general knowledge of the makeup of the test deck on the part of the subject. The resultant interdependency of targets/guesses, he argued, would affect the form of the distribution of scores, yielding a greater "spread" or "dispersion" about the mean than would be the case in truly random and independent sequences. Therefore, neither the normal distribution nor the binomial distribution (already suggested by Willoughby)[12] would be appropriate for this test situation.

No more than Willoughby did Kellogg like the appeal to a theoretical chance distribution; indeed he called for other tests of statistical significance which did not depend on any particular distribution, such as a chi-square contingency analysis, or even an empirical statistic to be calculated from the data itself. Behind the objection of these two psychologists to Rhine's procedure was more than a hint of the mistrust of the use of statistics to support claims they felt to be groundless. A more philosophical expression of this mistrust of the use of mathematics was offered to Rhine by the Harvard psychologist, E. G. Boring. By the fall of 1936, Rhine's work had attracted sufficient general attention to result in his being invited to address the psychology colloquium at Harvard on his work, which he did in late November. Both before and after his visit, Rhine and his host at Harvard, Boring, engaged in lengthy correspondence. Boring, while by no means prepared to dismiss Rhine's results

out-of-hand, was puzzled by them; he was particularly worried over Rhine's appeal to statistical
analysis to validate his claims to having demonstrated ESP.  To Boring, the very idea of an abstract "chance" distribution was meaningless, and
the mere comparison of the distribution of test
scores with such chance distributions provided the
scientist with no information about the purported
phenomena and certainly did not validate their
existence.  What was wanted was clear-cut experimental indication of what circumstances elicited
their manifestation.[13]

The early dialogue over statistical methods
had taken place in relative privacy and obscurity;
through 1936, parapsychology had remained limited
in its impact on the scientific community despite
the popular coverage.  Rhine  had neverthess begun
to correspond on technical matters with a number
of mathematicians and statisticians including
Thornton Fry of Bell Telephone Laboratories and
Churchill Eisenhart of University College London.
Nearer home, Rhine found a young mathematician at
Duke who, although not himself a statistician, was
willing to try to tackle the problems associated
with parapsychology and to serve as an advisor to
Rhine.  This was Joseph A. Greenwood, who eventually turned himself into a full-time statistician.
In the Spring of 1937, a forum for parapsychology
articles including discussions of the statistical
methods was provided by the founding of the Journal
of Parapsychology at Duke.  Indeed, in the initial
issue there was the first systematic, detailed and
comprehensive account of the Duke statistical procedures, jointly authored by Stuart and Greenwood.

In the Fall of 1937, Kellogg's criticisms of
parapsychology reached a wider audience through an
article in the semi-popular Scientific Monthly.[14]
A number of his earlier objections had already
been dealt with by Stuart and Greenwood: for
example, his contention that the "spread" or "dispersion" in a distribution of actual test scores
would be considerably greater than those accounted
for by either the normal or the binomial distribution.  By working out the most extreme case in
which two ESP decks were matched against each other,
they found that, while the spread or "variance"
was greater than in a stricly binomial distribution, the difference in the two distributions'

spread was scant, and would not significantly affect the determination of extra-chance significance
of the ESP results.[15]

But Kellogg produced further objections, mainly concerning the distribution of results in this
case--the "permutation matching distribution" as
he termed it.  He claimed that this distribution
yielded much higher probability values than did
the normal distribution for scores at its upper
end, and he published his own comparative tables
of probability values for the normal, binomial
and matching distributions to illustrate his contention.  In effect, Kellogg was now conceding
that the three distributions in question were
close enough to each other to be used interchange-
ably to evaluate test values near the mean; however, at the upper extreme (scores of 20 to 25),
the binomial and especially the permutation matching distributions would yield higher probability
values than would the normal distribution.

By the time this article appeared in Scientific Monthly, Rhine had secured more expert advice
in the person of the mathematician E. V. Huntington of Harvard.  Huntington had become interested
in the statistical issues of parapsychology and
had visited Duke in September.  Kellogg's
article only consolidated Huntington's support
of Rhine and he was able to bring two more mathematicians into the arena of controversy on the side
of parapsychology: his former student, Burton H.
Camp of Wesleyan University, then President of the
Institute of Mathematical Statistics, and Theodore
E. Sterne of the Harvard College Observatory.
These, along with Thornton Fry and, to a lesser
extent, Warren Weaver of the Rockefeller Foundation, came to constitute something of an external
consultant group for Rhine.  They were outraged
by the tone and substance of Kellogg's articles;
Huntington, in particular, vowed to support Rhine:

> . . . because the recent carping criti-
> cisms of some of your work make me feel
> that a substantial mathematical argument
> is after all the only thing that will
> silence some of these critics, in spite of
> the fact that such mathematical argument
> is really not necessary in your own research.[16]

Beyond exasperation with Kellogg, Huntington certainly felt a real interest in the mathematical problems which had been raised: in particular the need to produce a comprehensive and exact set of probability values for each score in the permutation matching hypothesis. For, while Kellogg had produced his own set of values for most of the possible scores, he had not indicated how he had calculated them; there was a necessity to redetermine them independently in order to test Kellogg's assertion about the probability values of the upper extreme of the distribution. This determination was a fascinating technical problem for its own sake to the mathematicians. On his return to Harvard, Huntington set to work deriving the distribution for the permutation matching hypothesis for the 3 x 3 and the 4 x 4 cases. Stimulated by Huntington's example, Sterne took up the 5 x 5 case--the ESP matching case--and by the first week in November he had worked out the first four moments of this distribution, the exact probability frequencies of the controversial higher scores, 21, 22, 23, 24 and 25, and very close approximations for scores 0 - 20. Huntington and Sterne immediately submitted two short articles containing these results to Science where they were published three weeks later.[17] Within the next month, two mathematicians, T. N. E. Greville at Michigan and Bancroft H. Brown of Dartmouth, independently computed the exact frequencies of all the scores from 0 - 20 of the matching distribution, thus completing the efforts of Huntington and Sterne and incidentally demonstrating the widening interest among mathematicians in the technical issues and problems associated with Rhine's ESP research.

This rapidly developing research was summarized in a survey by Stuart and Greenwood in the December, 1937 issue of the Journal of Parapsychology.[18] Utilizing Huntington's and Sterne's work they were able to carry out a detailed comparison of all three distributions which had been at controversy: the normal, the binomial and the matching. For very small numbers of test runs, the results of this comparison revealed non-trivial differences between the probability values derived from the normal distribution and those derived from the other two in the direction of lower

probability values (and hence greater significance
for C.R.'s) when computed on the basis of the normal distribution.  The author therefore suggested
that a slight adjustment be made in the C.R.
values taken as "threshold" for significance in
ESP tests.  In a general sense, then, Willoughby
and Kellogg had been technically correct in their
criticisms, but it was Rhine's associates who had
systematically and precisely demonstrated what the
relationships between these three distributions
were; and certainly the differences turned out to
be not nearly as serious as Kellogg had asserted
they were.

By the time this article appeared, parapsychology had received impressive public expressions of
confidence from mathematicians and statisticians.
The occasion was the holding of the AAAS meetings
in Indianapolis at the end of December, 1937,
where the American Mathematical Association and the
Institute of Mathematical Statistics also met.
Burton Camp, President of the latter organization,
presented Sterne's paper on the 5 x 5 matching
frequencies and issued a ringing statement of his
own to the press in support of statistical procedures used in parapsychology:

> Dr. Rhine's investigations have
> two aspects: experimental and statisti-
> cal.  On the experimental side mathema-
> ticians, of course, have nothing to say.
> On the statistical side, however, recent
> mathematical work has established the
> fact that, assuming that the experiments
> have been properly performed, the statis-
> tical analysis is essentially valid.  If
> the Rhine investigation is to be fairly
> attacked, it must be on other than mathe-
> matical grounds.[19]

The issuance of this statement brought to a climax
the activities of Rhine's mathematical supporters
in his behalf.  Throughout the Fall of 1937,
Huntington and Fry had given Rhine advice on how
to respond to Kellogg when they were doing the
actual response themselves.  Huntington, for example, had written a defence of the Duke laboratory's
statistical methods for <u>The American Scholar</u>[20] in
addition to his technical article in <u>Science</u>.
Moreover, it appears that he had a hand in the

formulation and issuance of Camp's statement along
with the Princeton statistician, S. S. Wilks.

In an interview for the <u>Washington Evening</u>
<u>Star</u> on January 2, 1938, Huntington made a reveal-
ing comment about his own motivation in coming to
the defence of parapsychology:

> No mathematician and no statistician
> has seriously complained. . . . One or two
> psychologists have published what they
> hoped would be devastating refutations.  I
> hate to see the prestige of mathematics
> and physics called into question.  I hope
> that those equally resentful with me over
> these attacks will join with me in regard
> to making some statement which will be of
> use to Dr. Rhine. . . . We should speak
> before any more discredit is brought on
> us.[21]

Huntington's sensitivity over "discredit" no
doubt reflected the uneasy status statistics
possessed in this country as a professional specialty despite the growing evidence of its utility
in a large number of fields.  While the field was
growing in size and had begun to develop profes-
sionarl structure in the 1930's (the founding of
the Institute of Mathematical Statistics in 1935
being an index of this), its academic recognition
continued to be unsatisfactory.  Harold Hotelling
testified on this point sarcastically in 1940:

> A university department of X, where X
> stands for economics, psychology, or any
> one of numerous other fields, begins to
> note toward the end of the pre-statistical
> era that some of the outstanding work in
> its field involves statistics. . . . The
> department therefore resolves that its
> students must acquire at least an elementary
> knowledge of the fundamentals of statis-
> tics. . . .
> The problem now arises of finding some-
> one to teach the new course.  Young Jones
> has already demonstrated a quantitative
> turn of mind in the course on Money and
> Banking, or in the Ph.D. thesis on which he
> has already made substantial progress, deal-
> ing with the Proportion of Public School

Yard Areas Surfaced with Gravel. He may
even recall having had a high school course
in trigonometry. His personality is all
that might be desired. He is white, Pro-
testant, native-born American. And so the
"Instructor to be announced" materializes
as Jones.[22]

Statistics, then, was still an underdeveloped and
even marginal field in the 1930's, caught between
the disinterest and even occasional contempt of
mathematicians and the often superficial and
amateurish manner in which it was learned and
applied by those who would use it in their own
research. Kellogg's handling of statistics was
no doubt to be placed in the latter category by
Huntington. It would seem that this perceived
threat from Kellogg helped to turn what had been
a two-way struggle between the parapsychologists
and some of the psychologists into a three-way
contest.

Camp's statement apparently expressed the
judgment of the assembled mathematicians and statisticians on the statistical issues. H. T. Davis
of Northwestern University agreed "that, on this
mathematical question, there was not a single dis-
senting voice at a meeting attended by several
hundred eminent mathematicians."[23] And, in fact,
the focus of criticism of ESP work by psychologists
shifted away from statistical techniques in 1938.

But this did not mean a sudden, dramatic or
decisive victory over the statistical issues as
Kellogg had formulated them. Kellogg, for one,
continued to pursue the matter during 1938 and
began his next article with a jibe at Camp's
statement:

> . . . a press release over the name of
> Prof. Burton H. Camp has served so
> thoroughly to befog the issues that it
> seems necessary to attempt a clearer formu-
> lation of the quantitative aspects of the
> problem.[24]

raising some of his original criticism yet again.
Moreover, a number of other psychologists had been
impelled by Kellogg's Scientific Monthly article
to launch their own criticisms of parapsychology

in the Fall of 1937.  Due in part to the inevitable
time-lag between the writing and the publication of
these articles, many of them actually reiterated
points already answered either by the statisticians
or by Stuart and Greenwood by the time they appeared and had the effect of seeming to prolong a
struggle which the protagonists themselves had
abandoned.[25]

   Moreover, some new statistical issues came
to the fore later in 1938 which had less to do
with statistical distributions than with the selection and compilation of experimental data.  One
was the question of "optional stopping," the ter-
mination of an ESP experiment at a point where the
overall score would yield extra-chance results,
rather than at the end of a predetermined number
of runs.  Another, even more general issue, was
whether there had been selection of the more
striking data and suppression of a mass of chance
results (and indeed, the question of whether this
might be legitimate under some circumstances).
The change in focus to optional stopping and data
selection was a part of the shift of discussion
in 1938 to issues of experimental method.  In one
sense, this shift was a tacit concession that
"the battle of the probabilities need hardly be
fought again."[26]  But these new criticisms were
also much more difficult for Rhine and his co-
workers to answer decisively because considerations
other than purely statistical ones were involved.
All the parapsychologist could do in answer to the
charge of data selection was to deny it (which
they did); for optional stopping, their response
was to undertake henceforth to make the predeter-
mination of test runs an essential component of
ESP experimental method.

   The controversy over statistical methods suggests some perhaps unexpected ways in which
Rhine's work was being perceived as unconventional
in the 1930's.  This first flurry of controversy
did not openly question the reality of ESP and
it saw nothing unusual about the nature of the
card guessing experimental situation itself.  Instead, it singled out as a minor matter the style
in which ESP had been presented in 1934.  Extra-
Sensory Perception, his monograph published by
the Boston Society of P sy c hi c Research, might
look to the psychical research community like a

"normal" scientific text than anything else in the field, given its tables of results, its statistical analysis, and its graphs of decline in performance. To psychologist critics, however, it was not really stylistically "right": experimental detail was not clearly spelled out, chronicle occasionally replaced analysis, and--as regards statistics--the combination of sketchy justification with exuberance of claims to "extra-chance success" made it appear quite unlike the normal text in tone and format. The critics tended to feel the same misgivings about the first two volumes of the Journal of Parapsychology.

Beyond this matter of mode of presentation, there was for psychologists another and even more interesting unconventional feature of Rhine's work, the important role assumed by statistics in validating his results. None too comfortable themselves with statistical analyses in the 1930's, Rhine's psychologist  critics were particularly uneasy about his using a theoretical "chance" distribution as the measure of statistical significance without giving the distribution of his own data or trying to validate (or better, generate) the chance distribution experimentally. All they saw at the heart of Rhine's claims was an abstract mathematical distribution, one moreover which they were not even sure was appropriate to this particular test situation. Hidden behind their objections, of course, lay an even more general skepticism of Rhine's claims to unprecedented success in demonstrating the existence of psychic abilities such as telepathy and clairvoyance. This attitude was the product of a long tradition of skepticism--and even hostility--to any claims of the paranormal on the part of most American psychologists, and was aggravated, in Willoughby's if not Kellogg's case, by inability to replicate Rhine's positive results. Hence, it seemed inevitable that Rhine's results would be explicable by some flaw in his method; in recognition of the centrality of the statistical argument to Rhine's claims, and at the same time because of their mistrust of it, Willoughby, Kellogg, and their successors concentrated their efforts on searching for flaws in the statistical procedures.

The perception of unconventionality in the application of statistics to this material was obviously not shared by Rhine; nor was it shared by other psychical researchers who had been using this method for a long time, nor, most importantly, was it shared by the mathematicians and statisticians with whom Rhine consulted and who contacted him. To these men, unconcerned with the broader experimental and ontological issues of ESP which established the context of psychologists' reactions, the statistical procedures of Rhine were essentially valid, and moreover left enough minor problems unsolved to be interesting.

We must of course bear in mind that the size of our sample is really too small to make conclusions about "conventionality" anything like secure. There were in 1937-1938 some 600 people in the United States who thought of themselves as professional psychologists. No more than 30 of these were actively enough interested in ESP to have left some trace of their reaction towards it, and no more than 10 took part in the first flurry of controversy over statistics. Our sample of sympathetic statisticians is still weaker. Still, what evidence is available suggests that in the first instance the "conventionality" or "unconventionality" of parapsychology was determined by the expectations and traditions of the particular scientific community which considered the subject, traditions which were concerned with matters of analytical technique rather than metaphysical issues. As a result, it was possible for the two groups to talk to rather than through one another and eventually to resolve the problem. Despite the original difference of viewpoint, despite the occasional acrimonious exchange, this remains perhaps the most rational and carefully defined debate that parapsychologists have ever had with their critics.

## References

[1] M. R. McVaugh and S. H. Mauskopf, "J. B. Rhine's Extra-Sensory Perception and Its Background in Psychical Research," Isis, 1976, 67: 161-189.

[2] Extra-Sensory Perception (Boston: Boston Society for Psychic Research, 1934).

[3]*Ibid.*, 32.

[4]*Ibid.*, 110.

[5]R. R. Willoughby to J. B. Rhine, August 1, 1934.  Rhine Papers, Department of Manuscripts, Perkins Library, Duke University, Durham, North Carolina.

[6]R. R. Willoughby to J. B. Rhine, August 2, 1934, Rhine Papers.

[7]R. R. Willoughby, "A Critique of Rhine's Extra-Sensory Perception," *J. Abn. and Soc. Psychol.*, 1935, 30:201; "The Use of Probable Errors in Evaluating Clairvoyance," *Char. and Personality*, 1935, 4:79-80.

[8]C. E. Stuart, "In Reply to Willoughby's Critique," *J. Abn. and Soc. Psychol.*, 1935, 30:384-385; "A Reply to Dr. Willoughby," *Char. and Personality*, 1935, 4:80.

[9]R. R. Willoughby to J. B. Rhine, September 8, 1936, Rhine Papers.

[10]C. E. Kellogg, "New Evidence (?) for 'Extra-Sensory Perception,'" *Sci. Monthly*, 1937, 45:332.

[11]C. E. Kellogg to J. B. Rhine, October 26, 1937, Rhine Papers.

[12]C. E. Kellogg, "Dr. J. B. Rhine and Extra-Sensory Perception," *J. Abn. and Soc. Psychol.*, 1936, 31:191-192.

[13]E. G. Boring--J. B. Rhine correspondence, Rhine Papers.

[14]C. E. Kellogg, *Sci. Monthly*, 1937, 45:331-341.

[15]J. A. Greenwood, and C. E. Stuart, "Mathematical Techniques Used in ESP Research," *J. Parapsychol.*, 1937, 1:211-212.

[16]E. V. Huntington to J. B. Rhine, October 10, 1937, Rhine Papers.

[17]E. V. Huntington, "Exact Probabilities in Certain Card-Matching Problems"; T. E. Sterne, "The Solution of a Problem in Probability," Science, 1937, 86:499-500 and 500-501 respectively (No. 26, 1937).

[18]C. E. Stuart and J. A. Greenwood, "A Review of Criticisms of the Mathematical Evaluation of ESP Data," J. Parapsychol., 1937, 1:295-304.

[19]Quoted by J. J. O'Neill, "In the Realm of Science: Extra-Sensory Perception Finds Champion in Mathematics If Not Psychology," Herald Tribune, 16 January, 1938 and at end of Vol. 1 of J. Para-psychol.

[20]"Is It Chance or ESP?," American Scholar, 1938, 7:201-210.

[21]Washington Evening Star, 2 January 1938.

[22]H. Hotelling, "The Teaching of Statistics," Annals of Mathematical Statistics, 11 (1940) quoted in Jerzy Neyman, "The Emergence of Mathe-matical Statistics," in On the History of Statis-tics and Probability, ed. D. B. Owen (N. Y.: Marcel Dekker, Inc., 1976), 179-180.

[23]Washington Evening Star, 2 January 1938.

[24]C. E. Kellogg, "The Statistical Techniques of ESP," Journal of Gen. Psychol., 1938, 19:383.

[25]Dael Wolfle, who wrote perhaps the ablest and most comprehensive of these critiques, ad-mitted subsequently that the parapsychologists' statistical procedures had been confirmed. D. Wolfle--J. B. Rhine, February 15, 1938, Rhine Papers.

[26]Kellogg as quoted in Extra-Sensory Percep-tion After Sixty Years, J. G. Pratt, J. B. Rhine et al. (New York, 1940), 229.

# 5

# Discussion

## On the Reception of
## Unconventional Scientific Claims

Marcello Truzzi

In speaking of what he termed the "essential
tension" in science, Thomas Kuhn has noted that:
"the successful scientist must simultaneously
display the characteristics of the traditionalist
and of the iconoclast."[1] It is this problem of
equilibrium that faces the scientific community in
its collective reception of unconventional
theories. The balance is a difficult one to put
into operation, and the history of science is
replete with examples of failure. In general
however, institutionalized science has tended to
be conservative and protective of its existing
bodies of currently accepted facts and theories.
Michael Polanyi has similarly noted that:

> The professional standards of science
> must impose a framework of discipline
> and at the same time encourage rebellion
> against it. They must demand that in
> order to be taken seriously, an investi-
> gation should largely conform to the
> currently predominant beliefs about the
> nature of things, while allowing that in
> order to be original it may to some ex-
> tent go against these.[2]

But Polanyi has defended the position of a strong
orthodoxy for science arguing as follows:

> Journals are bombarded with contributions
> offering fundamental discoveries in
> physics, chemistry, biology or medicine,
> most of which are nonsensical. Science
> cannot survive unless it can keep out

> such contributions and safeguard the
> basic soundness of its publications.
> This may lead to the neglect or even
> suppression of valuable contributions,
> but I think this risk is unavoidable.
> If it turned out that scientific dis-
> cipline was keeping out a large number
> of important ideas, a relaxation of its
> severity might become necessary.  But if
> this would lead to the intrusion of a
> great many bogus contributions, the
> situation could indeed become desperate.
> The pursuit of science can go on only
> so long as scientific judgments of
> plausibility are not too often badly
> mistaken.[3]

These sentiments by Polanyi are probably shared
by many critics of unconventional theories.  But
such an extreme defensive stance runs counter to
the fundamental openness of science to new data
and theories that most of us would value.  Charles
S. Peirce wrote that "Do not block the way of
inquiry"[4] should be the first rule of reason.
Many of us would agree that this must apply to
all reason in science.  In addition, many contemporary philosophers and historians of science
have emphasized the role of anomalies and puzzle
solving as the heart of science.[5]  Thus, it has
been argued, not only should we not suppress
anomalies, we should actively seek them out.  For
anomalies not only offer puzzles to solve, they
may constitute falsifications that force us to
expand and redevelop our cognitive maps of the
world.[6]

Ron Westrum has suggested that the problem
can often be likened to statisticians' concern
with Type I and Type II errors.[7]  The orthodox
concern is with avoiding a Type I error: thinking
there is variation when in fact there is not.  The
proponent of the unconventional claim, however, is
often concerned more about making a Type II error:
missing an important source of variation in the
world by mistakenly thinking nothing special is
happening.  Most scientists (as with most early
statisticians) are concerned with Type I errors.
They are more interested in the general pattern
they already have and don't want to mistakenly

acknowledge "unimportant" exceptions. But the unconventional theorist commonly feels the "exception" is highly important and fears that it will be missed. Thus, the proponent of acupuncture or psi thinks that the implausibility of such claims is secondary to their importance if they are true. These questions of significance may be related to broader philosophical concerns and may be part of what Polanyi calls the "tacit knowledge"[8] of science but which may also be viewed as part of what Harriet Zuckerman has referred to as a pre-public or "private phase of scientific inquiry."[9]

The problems surrounding the reception of unconventional science can perhaps be better understood by unpacking the central issues for each of these interlocked elements: <u>reception</u>, <u>unconventional</u>, and <u>science</u>. Let me consider these in reverse order.

## The Definition of Science

The basic issues surrounding the definition of what constitutes a science continue to be debated.[10] In at least a rough sense, made much rougher by recent work in the sociology of science, we can separate the social institution called science from the basic method of science (i.e., the attempt to intersubjectively validate or falsify systematic conjectures about the empirical world).[11] If one takes this separation seriously, scientific knowledge is defined not so much by its content as by its form. This perspective has special meaning for our common categorization of much unpopular thought as pseudoscience. As I have noted elsewhere,[12] this definition of pseudoscience as <u>methodologically flawed</u> science strongly suggests that there is some pseudoscience accepted as legitimate within the scientific community[13] while some methodologically proper work may be considered illegitimate by that community and thus gets labelled "pseudoscientific."[14] It should be noted that some forms of pseudoscience are simple charlatanry, as noted by P. H. Abelson in his complaints in an editorial in <u>Science</u>,[15] but many publicly labelled pseudosciences are honest attempts to gain scientific acceptance of alleged extraordinary events. I have suggested the term <u>proto-sciences</u> for such esoteric views, and I have

argued that belief systems can actually be taxono-
mized along a continuum from normal science at one
end to mystical occultism at the other.[16]

## The Unconventional Aspect

The recent scholarship in the history of
science has revealed a far more discontinuous process to us than is generally portrayed in our
textbooks.[17] Our notions of plausibility and
importance are often relative to our membership in
particular science subcultures.[18] This insulation
may have healthy consequences. Thus, early bio-
logists' ignoring of contemporary physicists'
arguments against the plausibility of evolution had
the happy ending that physics later changed its
estimate of the age of the sun so that the potential conflict never substantially emerged to inhibit the development of evolutionary theory.[19]
The point is, however, that different scientific
subcultures may have very different views of just
how extraordinary or anomalous a new claim is.[20]
Seymour Mauskopf's description of the statisticians'
view of parapsychology versus that of the psychologists (especially those in the specialty of perception) is a good case in point.[21] Acupuncture's
reception by dentistry and veterinary medicine
has been far more favorable than that by general
medicine.[22]

In addition to some relativity as to how extraordinary or plausible a new idea is, we should
also note that new claims can be highly specific
or very general, even to the point of claiming a
need for a whole new scientific specialty for its
study. This is well exemplified by the parapsychologists, many of whom view themselves not as a
specialty group within psychology but as a distinct science.[23] I have elsewhere argued that we
can differentiate cryptoscientific claims (ones
positing the existence of an extraordinary vari-
able, e.g., a unicorn) from parascientific claims
(ones positing the existence of extraordinary relationships between ordinary variables, e.g.,
astrobiological correlations).[24] Both crypto- and
para-scientific claims occur separately within all
sciences. Most of these constitute what Isaac
Asimov recently termed "endoheresies" or deviant
perspectives from within science.[25] These are

usually treated with some respect and courtesy by the orthodox scientist. But there are also "exoheresies" proposed by those outside of science, and these are commonly received with far less courtesy. One should probably distinguish two forms of exoheresy. One form consists of a scientist from one specialty area invading the domain of another. (This may also be viewed as a form of endoheresey relative to the total science community.) Wegener's background as a meteorologist made him a somewhat unwelcome intruder into the domain of geographers, and this probably had negative effects on the reception of his theory of continental drift.[26] It should also be noted, however, that the prestige structure of science is such that crossovers of research interest may be greeted differently depending upon the direction of the entry. Thus, some physicists' recent entrance into parapsychology (despite psychology's general rejection of psi claims) has probably enhanced the plausibility of psi's standing in the general scientific community.[27] Another version of such exoheresy may be cross-national. Thus, Chinese medicine's acceptance of acupuncture was widely viewed as an implausible treatment seeking entry from outside Western medicine.[28] But exoheresy from total or near total outsiders to the scientific community (a notable example being psychoanalyst-Physician Immanuel Velikovsky's astronomical and historical theories) have commonly been greeted with strong negative sanctions or ostracism, sometimes to our later embarrassment.[29] All of this strongly suggests that we should concern ourselves more with the methods employed by a proto-science and concentrate less on its substantive claims.

Unfortunately, recent work in the philosophy and history of science has further complicated our view of science's method. Facts do not simply speak for themselves; the presence of theories facilitates our acceptance of implausible facts; and Joseph Agassi has even pointed out that there may be times when we should ignore evidence in favor of an hypothesis.[30] Maier has even put forward a satirical law (following in the footsteps of Parkinson) based on his analysis of what is actually taking place in psychology, stating that "If facts do not conform to the theory, they must be disposed of."[31] These problems are clearly interrelated, and I can only hope future unpacking may lead us to clarify matters to the point of a solution.

## Factors in Reception

### By Scientists

A recent study by psychologist Michael Mahoney has confirmed what many of us practicing science strongly suspected.[32]    Scientists are not the paragons of rationality, objectivity, open-mindedness, and humility that many of them might like others to believe.  Though the American tradition in the sociology of science surrounding the work of Robert K. Merton[33] emphasizes the existence of scientific norms that should promote such virtues, the recent empirical work on scientists and their behavior, particularly by the British sociologists of science,[34] emphasizes the frequent absence of sanctions and the negotiable aspects of many of these alleged norms.  Much of scientific knowledge is perceived by these critics as socially negotiated.  They have argued that this is well demonstrated by examination of the reception of deviant theories and ideas within science.

### By the Public

A confounding of our problem is due to the possibility of direct appeal by some claimants of esoteric views to the mass media and the general public, often prior to submitting these to the science community.  Zuckerman has characterized this as "publicity seeking" that violates part of the etiquette within science.[35]  This has been a special problem for parapsychology whose funding has frequently come from extrascientific community sources.  Yet we too often neglect to remember that the exclusion of such theory groups from science may leave them little choice if they wish to continue.  This has sometimes resulted in public demand for the science community to respond to such publicized claims.  Unfortunately, the scientific community's response has sometimes been most imperfect, sometimes even been irresponsible, and seldom has been systematic.[36]

Seeking to institutionalize a responsive

mechanism for orthodox science to the more extreme and often publicly headlined claims of paranormal phenomena, a Committee was formed in 1976
to help the lay public better understand the de-
bates surrounding such claims.[37] This Committee
of critics and its publication (originally called
The Zetetic but now the Skeptical Inquirer) have
generated considerable media attention and may
have had some positive effects towards balancing
the usually one-sided publicity given claims of
the paranormal.

But there remains no balanced, systematic,
and institutionalized forum for fully debating
issues between the proponents and critics of claims
of anomalies.  Initiation of such a publication,
the Zetetic Scholar, is now underway, but its
success remains problematic.[38]  Its own reception
by the scientific community may tell us much about
the problem.  The social and intellectual matrix
is complex, but responsibility demands an attempt
be made to produce a more rational and efficient
means for adjudicating unconventional claims.
Science has little to gain by simply labelling its
proponents of unconventional ideas as "crackpots,"[39]
"pathological,"[40] or "pseudoscientists"[41] without
responsible examination of the evidence.  Such
authoritarian labelling is sometimes justified by
its alleged effect on a gullible public.[42]  But as
C. S. Peirce noted:

> the general public is no fool in judging
> of human nature; and the general public
> is decidedly of the opinion that there
> is such a thing as scientific pedantry
> that swells with complaisance when it can
> sneer at popular observations, not always
> wisely.[43]

Like any form of deviance within a social
group, unconventional ideas in science are seldom
positively greeted by those benefiting from con-
formity.[44]  But science's basic dependence upon
such innovations for its growth should remind us
of a special need for tolerance often absent in
the rest of society.  The "essential tension" remains with us, and we need to find better ways to
live with it.

## References

[1]Thomas S. Kuhn, The Essential Tension (Chicago), 277. The issues involved in the reception of unconventional ideas by science has a large literature. Some key works include: Bernard Barber, "Resistance by Scientists to Scientific Discovery," Science, 1961, 134:596-602; Edwin G. Boring, "The Validation of Scientific Belief," Proceedings of the American Philosophical Society, 1952, 96:535-539; Martin Gardner, "The Hermit Scientist," Antioch Review, 1950, 10:447-457; and L. Bernard Cohen, "Orthodoxy and Scientific Progress," Proceedings of the American Philosophical Society, 1952, 96:505-512.

[2]Michael Polanyi, "The Republic of Science: Its Political and Economic Theory," in his Knowing and Being (Chicago, 1969), 54-55.

[3]Michael Polanyi, "The Growth of Science in Society," ibid., 79.

[4]Charles Hartshorne and Paul Weiss (eds.), Collected Papers of Charles Sanders Peirce, Volume I: Principles of Philosophy (Cambridge, Mass.: 1965), 50.

[5]Cf., Willard C. Humphreys, Anomalies and Scientific Theories (San Francisco, 1968).

[6]Cf., Karl Popper, The Logic of Scientific Discovery (New York, 1959).

[7]Conversations with Professor Westrum during 1977.

[8]Cf., Michael Polanyi, Personal Knowledge (London, 1958) and "The Logic of Tacit Inference," in Polanyi, Knowing and Being, 138-158.

[9]Harriet Zuckerman, "Deviant Behavior and Social Control in Science," in E. Sagarin (ed.), Sage Annual Reviews of Studies in Deviance, Vol. I: Deviance and Social Change (Beverly Hills, 1977),124.

[10]The problem of demarcation between science and pseudoscience has largely developed from and in response to the seminal remarks of Sir Karl Popper in his The Logic of Scientific Discovery. On the evolving issues, see especially the relevant volumes in the Boston Studies in Philosophy series.

[11]An excellent introduction to this sociological separation can be found in Barry Barnes (ed.), Sociology of Science (Baltimore, 1972); and in R. K. Merton and J. Gaston (eds.), The Sociology of Science in Europe (Carbondale & Edwardsville, 1977).

[12]"Parameters of the Paranormal," in "Editorial," The Zetetic, 1977, 1:4-8.

[13]Psychiatry and the social sciences have been especially open to such criticism. On the former, see: E. Fuller Torrey, The Mind Game: Witchdoctors and Psychiatrists (New York, 1972); and on a more analytic level, Frank Cioffi, "Freud and the Idea of a Pseudo-Science," in R. Borger and F. Cioffi (eds.), Explanation in the Behavioural Sciences (New York, 1970), 471-499. In addition to the "Comment" by B. A. Farrell (pp. 500-507) and Cioffi's "Reply" (pp. 508-515), also see: Michael Martin, "Mr. Farrell and the Refutability of Psychoanalysis," Inquiry, 1964, 7:80-98; and V. L. Jupp, "Freud and Pseudo-Science," Philosophy, 1977, 52:441-453. On social pseudo-science, see: Pitirim A. Sorokin, Fads and Foibles in Modern Sociology and Related Sciences (Chicago, 1956); and Stanislav Andreski, Social Science as Sorcery (New York, 1972).

[14]Re the literature on popular demarcations between science and pseudoscience, see: M. Truzzi, compiler, "Crank, Crackpot, or Genius? Pseudoscience or Science Revolution? A Bibliographic Guide to the Debate," Zetetic Scholar, 1978, 1: 20-22.

[15]Philip H. Abelson, "Pseudoscience," Science, 1974, 184:4143. See also the letters related to this editorial in Science, 1974, 186:480-483.

[16]Marcello Truzzi, "Definitions and Dimensions of the Occult: Towards a Sociological Perspective," Journal of Popular Culture, 1972, 5:635-646.

[17]Stephen G. Brush, "Should the History of Science Be Rated X?" Science, 1974, 183:1164-1172.

[18]On the issue of plausibility, see: M. Truzzi, "On the Extraordinary: An attempt at Classification," Zetetic Scholar, 1978, 1:11-19.

[19]Cf., Loren Eisley, Darwin's Century (New York, 1961), 233-244.

[20]Group mechanisms that are related to such adoptions and rejection are nicely summarized (and quite applicable to scientific subcultures) in the chapter "Resistance to Change" and its section on "Cultural Barriers to Change" in Gerald Zaltman and Robert Duncan, Strategies for Planned Change (New York, 1977), 61-89.

[21]S. Mauskopf, "The Controversy over Statistics in Parapsychology, 1934-1938," in this volume. Paul Forman's discussion of the difference in German and British physics subcultures also illustrates such differences but across national lines. See "The Reception of an Acausal Quantum Mechanics in Germany and Britain," in this volume.

[22]E.g., cf., Alan M. Klide and Shiu H. Kung, Veterinary Acupuncture (Philadelphia, 1977).

[23]Re the scientific definition and domain of parapsychology, see the revealing introductory essay of Jan Ludwig in his anthology Philosophy and Parapsychology (Buffalo, 1978), especially 25-28.

[24]"Parameters of the Paranormal."

[25]Isaac Asimov, "Forward," in Donald Goldsmith (ed.), Scientists Confront Velikovsky (Ithaca, 1977), 8.

[26] In addition to Henry Robert Frankel's "The Reception and Acceptance of Continental Drift Theory as a Rational Episode in the History of Science," in this volume, see Chapter 20, "The Validation of Continental Drift" in Stephen Jay Gould, Ever Since Darwin: Reflections in Natural History (New York), 160-167.

[27] The entry of the so-called paraphysicists upon the scene has been met with mixed reactions by the regular parapsychologists.

[28] In addition to John Z. Bowers, "The Reception of Acupuncture by the Scientific Community: From Scorn to Degree of Interest," in this volume, see: Jacques M. Quen, "Acupuncture and Western Medicine," Bulletin of the History of Medicine, 1975, 49:196-205; and Joseph A. Kotaraba, "American Acupuncturists: The New Entrepreneurs of Hope," Urban Life, 1975, 4:149-177. On the early reactions, see: "Acupuncture in the Western World Up to a Century Ago" in Mark D. Altschule, Origins of Concepts in Human Behavior (Washington, D. C.: 1977), 153-163.

[29] E.g., cf., Alfred de Grazia, The Velikovsky Affair (New York, 1966).

[30] Joseph Agassi, Science in Flux (Dordrecht, 1975), Chapter 6: "When Should We Ignore Evidence In Favour of a Hypothesis?" 127-154.

[31] N. R. F. Maier, "Maier's Law," American Psychologist, 1960, 15:208-212.

[32] Michael J. Mahoney, "The Truth Seekers," Psychology Today, 1976, 60-65.

[33] For the best introduction, see: Robert K. Merton (Norman W. Storer, editor), The Sociology of Science: Theoretical and Empirical Investigations (Chicago, 1973). Others in the same tradition include Bernard Barber, Harriet Zuckerman, Norman W. Storer and Warren Hagstrom.

[34] Prominent here have been the writings of Barry Barnes, S. B. Barnes, Harry Collins, I. Mitroff, and Michael Mulkay. Of particular relevance to our discussion here, see: S. B. Barnes, "On the Reception of Scientific Beliefs," in Barry Barnes, Sociology of Science, 269-291.

[35] Zuckerman, 122.

[36] For an excellent discussion (and exemplification of the problem), see: Ron Westrum, "Scientists as Experts: Observations on 'Objections to Astrology,'" The Zetetic (now retitled The Skeptical Inquirer), 1976, 1:34-46 and the exchange following in this and the next issue.

[37] Cf., Kendrick Frazier, "Science and the Parascience Cults," Science News, 1976, 109:347-350.

[38] Cf., Boyce Rensberger, "Skeptics Criticized on Paranormal Issue," New York Times, Sunday, June 25, 1978, p. 21.

[39] E.g., Isaac Asimov, "CP," Analog Science Fiction, October 1974.

[40] I. Langmuir, "Pathological Science." Colloquium given at the Knolls Research Laboratory, December 18, 1953, transcribed and edited by R. N. Hall, General Electric Research and Development Center Report No. 68-C-035, April 1968.

[41] Obviously, the labelling of an unconventional theory and its followers as "counterfeit science" without proper expert evaluation of the evidence can itself be termed "pseudoscientific" procedure.

[42] Cf., M. Polanyi, Knowing and Being, 81.

[43] Hartshorne and Weiss, Volume VI: Scientific Metaphysics, 395.

[44]As the scientific enterprise has institutionalized and research programs have come to
compete for large resources and massive funding,
it seems likely that new forms of vested interests
will come to play important roles in the reactions
to innovative ideas and programs.  This has been
becoming a growingly recognized problem in some
areas of modern science.